# THE
# TAXIS
# OF
# THE
# MARNE

TRANSLATED FROM THE FRENCH BY HAROLD KING

*by*

*Jean*

*Dutourd*

SIMON AND SCHUSTER　　　NEW YORK　　　1957

*TO*

*LOUIS*

*NATHANIEL*

*ROSSEL*

GENERAL AND MINISTER OF THE COMMUNE,
SHOT AT SATORY ON NOVEMBER 28, 1871.

*Great in mediocre
circumstances,
superior to his
party and to his
adversaries, he was
devoured by a
country unworthy
of him.*

TO HIS MEMORY I DEDICATE THIS BOOK, WHICH IS
IMBUED WITH HIS SPIRIT AND HIS SOUL.    *J.D.*

# CONTENTS

## PART ONE
### MEMORIES AND RIGHTS

## CONTENTS

## PART TWO

### THE VICTIM CAST FOR
### THE LEADING PART

# CONTENTS

## PART THREE

### THE SPIRIT OF CONTRADICTION

# CONTENTS

# PART ONE

*Memories and*
*Rights*

VICE FOMENTS WAR; VIRTUE FIGHTS. WERE THERE
NO VIRTUE WE SHOULD HAVE PEACE FOREVER.

—Vauvenargues

# I

## *BRITTANY ON FOOT*

On June 25, 1940, at the age of twenty years and six months, after having been a soldier for fourteen days, I was taken prisoner. I have no unpleasant memories of this experience. After twenty years of childhood, school, and university, it made a change. For a week I marched across Brittany in the company of four other soldiers of my unit and an Alsatian sergeant by the name of Joseph, called Cepi. We wanted to steal a dinghy in some small port and sail down the coast to Bordeaux. We were very keen on this plan. As for me, I was so proud of my uniform that I wouldn't have left it in a ditch for anything in the world. Keeping it seemed all the more important to me, I believe, since we had been defeated. All six of us were luxuriating in friendship. The population helped and protected us. In one inn, a pretty girl served me beef stew with a great show of tenderness. I was only twenty, as I say: this tenderness pleased me and I did not think of taking advantage of it. Or rather I did think of it, but I did not do it.

Our group was very gay. We were no longer quite soldiers, but we had kept our arms and steel helmets. Each of us had a revolver which perhaps we might have occasion to use. Crossing Brittany on foot, observing the disorganization in the region, the flight of the population, the stampede of the authorities, and even the rout of inanimate things (we saw mattresses abandoned in open fields, which is not where mattresses belong), I thought that France was strained like a rope and that the rope must slacken or break. I remember making the comparison; it was running around in my head during the whole of my journey. The rope slackened, to the great relief of everybody, when Pétain announced on the wireless that he had asked for an armistice.

# II

## COURAGE

What would have happened if the rope had snapped? I did not dare imagine. That France could burst like a soap bubble passed my understanding. Not only was I young and without experience, but I was also suffering from that natural defect of youth, timidity; I couldn't bring myself to conceive of complete over-throw and total destruction. The fact is that we lacked desperation. What we should have had was the desperation of Finland. We were not up to the militiamen of the Army of the Loire or to the Federates.

In certain circumstances a man must be ready to die on the spot. I did not know this. Cepi, who was a traveling salesman in civilian life, did not know it either, and in any case he didn't have the qualities essential in a leader. He was a decent fellow, not stupid, and quite resourceful, who soon put us at our ease by saying, "You don't have to call me sergeant any longer. We're all equal now. Call me Cepi." As he was seven or eight years older than the rest of us, he believed it was his duty to save the lives of my four companions and myself—which, incidentally, he did. He led us to Auray, where we were all six taken prisoner without a scratch.

Duty obviously demanded that we should stop in some village, build a barricade, and fire on the first German motorcyclists that turned up. Five stalwarts and a sergeant in every village of Brittany, and the face of the war would have been changed. There was certainly no "Britanny redoubt," but what of it? We should have held the Morbihan, the Finistère, and the Côtes-du-Nord for a week. In a week an army corps could have been reconstituted some-where and sent to the rescue. And even if no army corps had come, that week would have been worth living. Not all of us would have died, and honor would have been saved. The recruits of Brittany, with their two weeks of training, would have had the pleasure of being called "the flower of French youth." By 1940 we French had not astonished the world for a long time. But nobody thought of such a thing, and I, who am moralizing here and amusing myself at rewriting history, did not think of it either until two or three years later.

Courage, like artistic inspiration, begets itself. It isn't very difficult to act courageously when you've already done so once, just as it isn't so hard to write the hundredth page of a book as the first. In June 1940 I was not courageous, but I could have become so with the greatest of ease. It would have been enough to be courageous once. If Sergeant Cepi had led us into danger instead of skillfully leading us away from it, we should quite naturally have become heroes.

# III

## GENERALS

Apparently the hour for courage had not struck. France had forgotten the word. The government had even lost our national tradition of martial eloquence. Shades of Danton and Gambetta! All they could think of to arouse us was the slogan "We shall win because we are the strongest."

Base words, the exhortation of a mean government to a cowardly people. They should have painted on the walls in great letters, "We shall win because we are the bravest." Besides being nobler, it would also have been truer, for war is not a question of arithmetic. Was the government afraid that if it mentioned bravery the country would laugh in its face? Certainly it is possible to be *crushed* by an enemy greatly superior in numbers or in equipment, but that was not what happened to us. On the contrary: we were in fact the strongest. If God is on the side of the big battalions, he was on our side, and all the more so as the enemy was not worth anything. Our fathers, the poilus who pulverized the redoubtable army of the Kaiser, would have made short work of these young Nazi guttersnipes trembling in their cardboard fortlets. Yes, the only thing our big battalions lacked was courage, and courage was a word nobody even whispered. It might have been some shameful disease. The war was not lost on September 3, 1939; it was lost in the months that followed. And hard as I search, I can find only one reason for our defeat: stupidity and cowardice. The generals were stupid, the men did not want to be killed. These two things often go together. Troops know that an idiot has no right to ask them to get themselves killed. We were the strongest and we did not conquer. What was missing was virtue.

The French generals had the instruments of victory in their hands. What nobody realized was this: they were longing to change their profession. They did not like war. They had mistaken their vocation. As another soldier, their spiritual father, guessed so well, their real inclination was for quieter occupation: accountant, postmaster, colonial administrator, lawyer, prefect, police commissioner, high-court judge—they secretly longed to be civil servants. No more army, for the love of Heaven! No *responsibilities!*

I feel a personal grudge against these peace-loving generals. Mistaking their own vocation, they sabotaged mine. I burst with rage when I look back at myself, I who am thrilled by the slightest flourish of trumpets, I who find tears in my eyes when I read *Honneur et Fidélité,* I who am breathless at the thought of the wooden hand of Captain Danjou, bowled over by the statue of Marshal Ney holding out his sword near the site of the old "Bal Bullier," transfixed by *La Marseillaise* of Rude, and overcome by the flame under the Arc de Triomphe. If those sorry men had not ruined my career in 1940 I would have been a knight of the Legion of Honor (a Legion of Honor worth belonging to) at the age of twenty, and a captain in the finest infantry in the world. The damned scoundrels!

# IV

## *THE BOX OF MATCHES*

It is a curious sensation, calculated to sear the soul forever, to find oneself at the age of twenty caught up in a national catastrophe. Does anyone today still remember the France of 1938? I was then a penniless, middle-class youth, and France seemed to me an impressive community: marmoreal, eternal. In it I was rather in the position of a young girl of good family in 1880 who wants to become an actress against the wishes of her father, a Supreme Court Judge.

Suddenly the family collapses: the mother runs away with a band leader;

the brother goes to prison for fraud; after a scandal which leads to his suicide the Supreme Court Judge is revealed as a homosexual. The young girl is overwhelmed with grief, no doubt about that, but at the bottom of her desolation she perceives a light which has just been kindled and which shines for her alone—the light of freedom. She will enter a school of dramatic art, like any shopkeeper's daughter. She has descended to the delicious level of the rabble, from which she will fly toward far greater heights than those of the orthodox middle class. For this young girl to know happiness, her social cell had first to be destroyed.

I was very conscious of the lack of proportion between the happenings of the time and my own ideas. And for this defeat to provide me with my sentimental education was comparable to felling all the forests in the Urals to make one box of matches. However, the forests *were* felled, and for myself at any rate there was this precious box of matches.

I confess that on the byroads of Brittany, with my four comrades and Cepi, I felt very happy. Chains were imprisoning my country, but my own shell was splitting and crumbling. I was leaving the middle class, I was abandoning my childhood. I had stepped out of the frame of my life. Nothing familiar any longer struck my eyes. I was traveling in a countryside I had never seen, in the company of men I had not known three weeks earlier, dressed as I had never been before, and placed in an unimaginable situation. Defeated, my country had sunk to the level of a rabble nation. We were no better than the unfortunate peoples of Central Europe or South America, at the mercy of the first invader, not lacking in dignity perhaps, but slaves and prostituted for all that. At the moment when we were about to suffer an unguessed-at tyranny, every opportunity was open to me.

I made hardly any use of these opportunities. I was too busy enjoying the sensation of freedom to make use of freedom itself. And then, the road was too straight: such roads never lead anywhere. A man needs difficulties if he is to accomplish anything, if he is to fulfill himself. I would gladly have done great things, but I lacked imagination. If only someone had said to me, "Be a hero." But nobody did. Rather the opposite. Where I was, heroism was discredited, and a man appealing to it would have seemed ridiculous.

From the doors of their cottages the peasants watched France go by. She had turned into a multitude of fleeing soldiers with a shifty look in their eyes, completely absorbed in a desire for personal safety. What were these soldiers thinking about, these soldiers who had seen their officers take flight in livid-colored Citroëns? In their own way they were desperate, but it was not a good way. They had been thrown back on their own. A rout chemically decomposes an army, it isolates its various elements; thus the armies of 1940 disintegrated into thousands of individuals. The armies, those great souls animated by the elementary passions of friendship, abnegation, and desire for glory, once again split up into little souls, into self-contained particles plagued by the paltry problems of how to survive, how to get away safely, how to eat, how to steal a bicycle or scrounge civilian clothes. War draws men out of themselves: in battle the prudent become daring, the miserly lavish, and even cowards display valor. To defend one's country is no mean task. To fight by the side of the brave makes the most sordid man generous. Men who were ready, despite themselves, to cast off their mediocrity were thrown back on it by the collapse of 1940. Although they went on wearing uniforms, the soldiers had become civilians again. Instantly, all the ideas of civilian life regained control of their hearts.

# V

## *CAMBRONNE ON THE CHEAP*

I do not wish to be misunderstood. I do not say that French soldiers between September 1939 and May 1940 dreamed of glory or that they piously and solemnly prepared to win. I do not even say that they entertained slight illusions. The French army was poorly organized and inert. Worthy descendants of the soldiers of 1870, the soldiers of 1939 became for the second time an "army of Darius." After Darius-Badinguet, Darius-Daladier! In addition, a certain number of gaiter buttons were missing. The gunners settled down in the Maginot Line like apartment-house janitors, trailing about the corridors in slippers, playing innumerable games of cards under the silent guns, yawning from morning to night. The French army became so bored in its quarters that actors and singers were sent in to entertain it. The "Army Theater" was the only operation which was carried through satisfactorily. As the months went by, the war more and more began to look like a huge picnic that was smothering our frontiers in greasy paper and sausage skins. Was war nothing much more than a bit of uncomfortable camping? Across the lines, the German soldiers sent the French friendly messages over their loudspeakers. To salve their consciences the French, through their own loud-speakers, shouted back, *"Merde."* * Their frequent use of this word enabled the French soldiers to act Cambronne on the cheap. The word running down the whole line filled the Parisian papers with delight. They saw in the frequency of its use a barometer of the morale of our troops. Men who shouted *merde* so promptly were bound to fight like lions—when the time came.

Pessimistic as I am, I cannot believe that the French soldiers were happy during those eight months. First of all, waiting is never pleasant. What would happen at the end of this waiting? Would it be slaughter or demobilization? Eight months is too long to get ready for a tragedy; it gives time for the flowering of a most pernicious idea—the idea of a miracle. This notion must have begun to spread in the spring of 1940, after the rigors of the Alsatian winter. The blue line of the Vosges hills takes on pretty pink colors under the rays of a watery spring sun, and no doubt the weather

* *Translator's note:* General Pierre Cambronne commanded one of the last resisting units of the Old Guard of Napoleon at the battle of Waterloo. Surrounded and challenged to surrender, he is said to have replied, *"Merde,"* or "To hell with you." According to Littré, he said, "The Guard dies; it does not surrender."

made it difficult to accept the possibility of death. During the winter you are busy keeping warm. The sky is heavy, night falls fast, and all this communicates dark thoughts and undermines hope. Which is excellent. But spring penetrates violently into the half-open soul. What miracle was being prepared for us by our humanitarian generals and the paternal government which had so skillfully saved us at Munich? And what about the French way of life, its comfort and happiness? It was inconceivable that the cowardly, good-natured regime of the Third Republic, so totally devoid of poetry, would suddenly collapse in some Biblical upheaval. Happiness is surely not lost so easily. The very word *happiness* was synonymous with France; since for so many years we had been constantly told that France was eternal, too.

Behind the French front the vast memories of 1914 floated by like shadows. The jolting ghosts of the taxis of the Marne, sufficently ancient-looking not to be ridiculous, emerged from the past. There would again be taxis springing up at the eleventh hour, at the ultimate moment. It would be the taxis of the Seine; yes, the Seine perhaps this time, or even the Loire. Soldiers would clamber into them— their haversacks stuffed with gingerbread and their stomachs filled with red wine—and would head straight for Berlin. "We shall win because we are the strongest," the posters stupidly proclaimed. If that were true, there was no point in worrying. France was an enormous tortoise, head and feet carefully withdrawn inside its shell. Let the *Boches* come. You start the shooting, you Nazi gentlemen! Your bombardment will bounce off our concrete walls and fly back into your ugly mugs. When you are properly tired and hungry we shall show ourselves and stage our military walk-over. It is quite easy to win a war when one is strongest: all that's necessary is to wait.

As a matter of fact, I believe that these soldiers, who were living like civilians on holiday, were unconsciously hoping that at the end of their long wait they would be offered the chance to be heroes. No army, not even Darius's army, can live in a state of complete abjection. Dishonored arms become insufferable. To dress men in uniform and then abandon them to inaction is a mockery. It is transforming war, a grave and terrible thing, into a masquerade. When the French were mobilized, some left gaily, others sadly. But the most defeatist believed they were going off to fight; the most cowardly did not hope that they were being invited to eight months of carnival, that for 250 days they were simply going to eat big meals and see free shows.

# VI

## *A GREAT SOUL*

People always refuse to believe that governments can be stupid and blind. The feeling is, "They must know . . ." But no, they do not know. In 1940 they did not know that the Maginot Line could be outflanked through Belgium or overflown with planes. They did not know that our heavy artillery was at Valence and our tanks in the Pyrenees. They did not know that inaction is the worst enemy of an army in the field. Naturally, a government is not stupid in the way an individual is. It can even happen that a collection of very clever men may produce a stupid government. That is because politics calls for something more than a nimble wit. It calls for a broad view and for force of character, two things you do not learn at a French law school or university. Only great souls do great things. That phrase "great soul" turns up over and over again in Stendhal's life of Napoleon. What historian other than Stendhal has perceived the greatness of Napoleon's soul? Yet there lies the whole key to his character. Louis XIV despite his narrow-mindedness and Mazarin despite his knavishness were also great souls. But who would dare talk of the great souls of the Messrs. Chautemps and Daladier, or of General Gamelin and President Lebrun?

There was a great soul somewhere in the offering, but he was tied down in the promotion rosters of the army; he was condemned to vegetate in garrison towns, with an occasional minor command to relieve the monotony. It needed nothing less than the disintegration of the nation to liberate this great soul from his bonds. He faced the catastrophe which had left the nation dazed with the most extravagant and yet the most sensible action. He displayed what had been totally lacking in French politics since 1920: imagination.

# VII

## *JACK-OF-ALL-TRADES*

The reader will have recognized General de Gaulle and his famous appeal of June 18, 1940. But I am proceeding too quickly; let me go back to the month of February. What was the government doing while the soldiers were eating their heads off? It was reducing to the ranks corporals guilty of asking themselves, in letters to their sweethearts, what

18

the chances were of victory for an army advancing on foot at two and a half miles an hour in the face of German columns moving forward at the speed of trucks. It was demobilizing twenty-two-year-old conscripts and drafting veterans of the expedition to China. It was posting bills on the walls of burgled houses: "Looting is punishable by death." It was discussing a Parliamentary proposal dealing with the supply of wine to army canteens. It passed legislation dealing with the sacred rights of the sons of victims of the previous war. It censured the newspapers right and left. It repeated without end, "All is going well; all is for the best; above all, do not be afraid; there is no danger." A real job of leadership! A job complicated by minutely detailed preparations for campaigns (which never took place) in Syria and Finland.

The government was also thinking about a miracle. It looked for this miracle the way a mathematician looks for the roots of an equation. Finally it found the unknown quantity. It was called Narvik,* but it

* *Translator's note:* Narvik, a small iron-ore port in northern Norway, was captured by Allied forces (British, French, and Polish) on May 29, 1940, and evacuated by them eleven days later, on June 8. The departure of the Allied troops from Narvik, without a shot's being fired at them by the enemy, was the end of an attempt started early in April of that year to prevent the Germans' taking all Norway, or at any rate to preserve an Allied foothold in the country, from which the King of Norway could exercise his sovereignty. (The Germans had occupied Oslo and other principal towns of Norway on April 9.)

was a miracle for mediocrities, and a false miracle at that. Narvik was all right as part of the reassuring nonsense of poor Giraudoux's propaganda —the iron-ore route has been cut, the Germans will be brought to their knees by starvation, the war can be won with a handful of men. Briefly, it was the little man's know-how applied to history. Other times, other miracles—the taxis of the Marne had the quality of greatness; they symbolized an exploit comparable to that of Leonidas. Narvik was comparable to an amateur inventor's exhibition. It consisted of opposing power and science with the traditional skill of a French jack-of-all-trades.

It is not astonishing that an idea like Narvik excited the cabinet ministers of that time. It was exactly the kind of idea to seduce brilliant intellects: it had the double advantage of being paradoxical and mean; in other words, it surprised but did not frighten. At little cost it enabled the ministers to delude themselves into believing that they were gambling and being audacious. With one hundred francs you could break the bank. What glory in store! It is strange that the wording of the posters was not changed and that Frenchmen did not read on their walls, "We shall win because we are the cleverest." In France, such a slogan would have caught on. But the bank was not broken, and we lost our hundred francs.

In Brittany in June 1940 I saw half a dozen men who had escaped from

Narvik. God knows how they got stranded in Brittany. They wore smart, short topcoats lined with sheep's wool which everybody else envied. Gloomy and reserved, they looked at us with contempt. They had captured a town only to abandon it the next day. They had been forced to run away from their own victory—a rare feat in the annals of war. We surrounded them with respect and consideration, as if they were sick and grumpy uncles. They were men, we were not. At least they had been under fire. Today the respect we paid them seems to me highly revealing; it was the tribute paid by our cowardice, by men who were very glad to be rid of the war, to those who had done some fighting for the sake of honor. The truth is that if our minds and hearts had not been completely perverted, we should have hated these victors in flight, we should have given them the same contempt we showed to our elders. Rage at being captured without having shown the measure of our courage ought to have made us unjust and fierce. After all, we had been deprived of the pleasure of fighting.

# VIII

*THE SQUARE
OF LOST
VICTORIES*

A square in Paris not far from the Boulevard Haussmann was recently renamed. It is now called Narvik Square. Suppose that three generations ago, in 1880, the Paris Municipal Council had called someplace in the capital of France the "Rue de Gravelotte," or the "Boulevard Saarbrücken," or the "Avenue de Reichshoffen"! What an outcry there would have been! Yet Saarbrücken was captured by our troops the way Narvik was. Gravelotte was a French victory—the enemy lost 17,000 men and retreated everywhere. At Reichshoffen we fought with desperation—the Horse Guards of General Duchesne got themselves killed as bravely as the cavalry of Caulaincourt had in Russia fifty-eight years earlier. And they were not killed for nothing. Marshal MacMahon, who was notorious for his stupidity, saved the army by throwing in this cavalry, and thereby showed himself a much better strategist than anything the French Staff College produced between 1920 and 1940.

But when all is said and done, and despite the legend, inevitably invented afterward, of its having been a glorious defeat, the war of 1870 was generally considered in France as a war that had been lost. "Think of it ever, speak of it never," people repeated, after Gambetta. Wise words, with which a dignified people and a still serious-minded government were deeply imbued.

Between 1872 and 1914 there were always enough hard-headed people to remind themselves of the fact that our defeat, despite some superb actions in the field, despite some clever moves by General Faidherbe and General Chanzy, and despite the siege of Paris, was a shameful defeat caused by the stupidity of the government and the general staff.

Of all the military actions of 1940 Narvik is perhaps the one that carries the most painful memories. What is more bitter than a victory lost? If the Municipal Council of Paris had a spark of pride or a bit of character, it would now rechristen its Narvik Square and call it "The Square of Lost Victories." A tablet could be inscribed, as used to be done in Paris and is still done in the provinces: "This square has been so named in memory of the capture of Narvik, a victory which proved absolutely useless due to the stupidity of the French High Command in 1940." Let us at last humiliate them, these doddering numskull generals of ours, these reincarnations of the gilded old fogies of Austria and Prussia, around whom the illiterate colonels of Napoleon made rings with the greatest of ease. Let us create a purgatory for chiefs who know nothing but how to lose wars. The Committee of Public Safety * was not so gentle: it cut off the heads of incapable generals. That encouraged the others to gain victories. Brunet did not know how to fight; his execution may well have taught Kléber his heroism. Since 1939, at least thirty generals have deserved to be shot. The lesson would not have been lost on everybody; dead, those thirty would have saved the lives of many others.

# IX

## *THE GLORIFICATION OF FAILURE*

For what reason does our government organize triumphs for defeated generals when they return from their disasters? Truly a tender mother, this government. It wants to console at all costs. The explanation, no doubt, is that

* *Translator's note:* The Committee of Public Safety was nominated by the French Convention (Parliament) on April 6, 1793. It was the governing center of the country and used the system known as "The Terror," which for them was no more than martial law used for achieving military success.

the failures of the generals excuse the failures of the government: generals in full flight are the delight of incapable ministers. "Lions led by asses," it was said of the army in 1870. Where have the lions been the past fifteen years?

A complete theory about present-day France could be developed under the title "Failure Considered as Success." This glorification of failure is not new. It turns up infallibly in tired societies. Saint-Simon described it very well in his memoirs when dealing with the last years of the reign of Louis XIV. "At our age," the king said to Marshal Villeroi, returning from his defeat at the battle of Ramillies, "one is no longer lucky." And everybody, it appears, was stupefied to see the king still showering the marshall with favors.* The reason was that Louis XIV grew fainthearted as he grew old, and success scared him. He could no longer forgive it except in the case of Villars, who was slightly mad and rather dishonest.

To get to the point of priding oneself on one's failures, in the name of some kind of romanticism of bad luck, made fashionable by some fool in government office, is an astonishing piece of buffoonery. The cult of martyrdom and of the glory of defeat has never been so widely celebrated as it has been since 1945. This is not the philosophy of an unhappy people;

* In May 1956 General N——, defeated in Indo-China, became a member of the Superior Council of War.

it is the philosophy of imbeciles. People have the kind of romanticism they deserve. French opinion, manufactured by successive governments, recalls the stupid convict who had tattooed on his chest, "They call me Unlucky Charlie." Before talking of a glorious defeat, one should remember that a defeat often indicates more stupidity on the part of the vanquished than intelligence on the part of the victor, and that there is no glory in being stupid. Almost all wars, and particularly that of 1939–1940, proved this. Courage or cowardice, arms and numbers, are certainly important factors, but they are secondary. What loses wars first and foremost is stupidity.

Everyone is familiar with the remark of the Frenchman who on his first visit to London crossed Trafalgar Square and then arrived at Waterloo Bridge. "How odd," he exclaimed. "In this city, streets are given the names of defeats in battle." Soon this amiable Frenchman will no longer have to cross the Channel: a walk through Paris will do. After their "Narvik Square," the Municipal Council might as well rechristen some highway "Waterloo Avenue." In the way of lost battles Waterloo is rather better than Dien Bien Phu, which name has actually been given to a class of cadets of Saint-Cyr.* A

* What respect can the young soldiers of the Dien Bien Phu class have for the chiefs who gave them this name of defeat? Do they themselves not feel soiled by the shame their elders are handing on to them? What respect can they feel for such and such a general came to inspect them who has nothing to offer but

few more years of misfortune, a few more miracles of strategic idiocy, and a decree will be issued replacing the Church of Our Lady of Victories by the Church of Our Lady of Defeats. Such humility would be highly Christian.

Curious discoveries are sometimes made in the obscure works of grammarians. Who knows M. André Moufflet? This excellent professor some ten years ago wrote a volume entitled, without much attempt at originality, *To the Rescue of the French Language*. On page 129 there is this admirable passage, striking in its penetration and its aptness:

> After the war of 1870 a deplorable convention led to numerous developments on the theme *gloria victis*. The typical hero was no longer the French soldier victorious, the soldier of Arcole, of Austerlitz, of Wagram, but the soldier who *falls* in protecting the retreat of his comrades. It is a curious thing that although after that time French soldiers conquered Tonkin and Morocco and won the war of 1914–1918, yet the habits of speech contracted between 1870 and 1914 have left their trace. Too often the hero is the unhappy or unlucky soldier.
>
> When people begin to say that troops resisted *heroically* or that they deployed prodigies of *heroism,* it means things are going badly.

an example of cowardice and stupidity? It is true that youth is credulous: it salutes the uniform. In its eyes the uniform and glory are one. After all, the general does have a few medals on his chest which show that there were moments in his life when he was less lamentable than usual. The young cadets of Saint-Cyr do not yet know that the Legion of Honor is won by licking the boots of Cabinet ministers.

This use of "hero" is more than a figure of speech, more than an inappropriate or mistaken use of words. It becomes and betrays a sickness of character.

M. Moufflet does not mince his words. He writes black on white: sickness of character. With his *gloria victis* he puts his finger directly on the fundamental problem of contemporary France: the hero versus the martyr, the failure regarded as victory. Seven or eight years ahead of time, he announces the Dien Bien Phu class at Saint-Cyr; he prophesies that a monument will be erected. to the Unknown Prisoner; he conjures up the thousand and one aspects of French life which consecrate incompetence, incapacity, negligence, and disorder; he describes the demented indulgence, the perversion of common sense, the inverted. morals, the absurd nonconformity hallowed by the State itself which the French nation has displayed since its reverses. To accept disappointment with equanimity and to half welcome misfortune are characteristic traits of old age. Almost invariably they are found in creatures too aged and too weak to exercise influence on the world.

I don't share Louis XIV's indulgence of defeated generals. I can't afford such indulgence. When kings fell on evil days they did not necessarily fall from their thrones. But the Republic is crumbling, and the world is tearing at France as if she were a toothless old lion dying by the wayside. In me, an insignificant civilian, defeated generals inspire nothing but contempt. I want these functionaries, whom I pay, to know their business. That is to say, I want them to win wars. Or else let them be dismissed. I am not alone, I believe, in thinking this way. I want the contempt in which the country holds its generals to be officially manifested to them. I want them to consider the uniform they wear as dishonored until further notice. Let us change these self-satisfied and self-important generals into worried soldiers, eaten up with shame and eager to redeem themselves. There is no historic fatality: one man of genius and ten men of honor could restore France in six months. It may be objected that one of the facts of the situation is that these so ardently desired eleven persons do not turn up, and that therein lies the fatality of history. And yet these eleven men do exist. They are somewhere. They are locked up inside the community, as though they were behind the door of a safe. Revolutions blast open such doors very easily. In 1788 there was not a single man of genius in the French administration or in the French army. A year later men of genius were being scooped up by the bucketful.

# X

## FIELD
## MARSHALS

Since we are dealing with generals, let us admire in passing (so that someone at least will have done so) the creation of French field marshals after the victory of the Allies—the victory that was so little of our own making. Promotions to the rank of field marshal after a defeat are not so common as not to merit a moment's consideration. In our day not much is needed to obtain the highest military dignity of France. One campaign, a single feat of arms by a colonel in the field, and there you have a field marshal, so rare have good officers become. Faidherbe and Chanzy * did every bit as much as Juin and Leclerc. They were not made field marshals for all that. They were unlucky: President Grant, Queen Victoria, and Czar Alexander II did not join hands against Bismarck.

* *Translator's note:* General Louis Faidherbe (1818–1889) was commander of the Army of the North of Napoleon III in France's war against Prussia in 1870, which ended with a French defeat. General Alfred Chanzy (1823–1883) scored a victory over the Prussians in 1870 at Coulmiers, and later led a French retreat from Vendôme.

# XI

## *DYING FOR DALADIER*

Certain colonels are called the fathers of their regiments. The government of 1939–1940 was the father of its army, but an unworthy father, an easygoing father, one of those many benevolent fathers whose indulgence leads their children to the gallows. One does not send soldiers into battles telling them there is no risk. That is a fraud, the same kind of deception as telling one's children that cod-liver oil has a delicious taste. We really had a very poor lot of statesmen. They did not even know that you can ask anything of the people. These ministers were so little persuaded of their superiority, or rather so conscious of their baseness, that they dared demand nothing. In 1938 M. Marcel Déat said he "refused to die for Danzig." I am convinced that in 1939 the then Premier, M. Édouard Daladier, a man of intelligence, said to himself in the silence of his office in the Rue Saint-Dominique, with that keen sense of the ridiculous that high office had not made him lose, "I cannot after all order the hundred and twentieth regiment of the line to die for Daladier; they would laugh in my face." M. Édouard Daladier did not identify himself with France. Despite his full powers, his decree laws, his distinguished Parliamentary past, and his "victory" at Munich which had made of him a monarch as absolute as Hitler, he continued to consider himself the humble representative of his Parliamentary constituency in the Vaucluse and to envisage his career as a purely personal matter. That was modesty indeed. Too much of it, in fact. M. Daladier ought to have been the voice of France, but he spoke only in the name of M. Daladier, the Radical and Radical-Socialist Party and the anticlerical Vaucluse, all interesting, worthy names, no doubt, but with little relation to the circumstances and far beneath what *at that time* was expected of the President of the Council of Ministers of the French Republic.

# XII

## *THE LION*
## *AND*
## *THE POODLE*

The fact that Jean Giraudoux, who did not even believe what he wrote, was catapulted into the post of Commissar for Information and Propaganda when the war started, explains a great deal about the period. Such a choice for such a position shows that those in charge were thoroughly determined to be up to date, were at last stoutly decided to make use of talent and competence. It also shows that cabinet ministers ought to have a modicum of literary taste or at least have read a book or two. If before appointing Giraudoux as France's wartime propaganda chief, they had taken a look at the works of the author of *Intermezzo*, they might perhaps have realized that this man of letters had no depth to him; they might have noticed that he says everything, in the prettiest manner in the world— everything, that is, except the essential. A writer who in his work never comes to grips with anything essential is a frivolous man, a lightweight. In time of war, it is the essential that matters. Giraudoux in charge of propaganda could invent a few pleasing and ingenious things; he could not possibly get to the heart of the problem.

Paul Claudel is the man they ought to have appointed. He was of a stature equal to the situation. He would have found words capable of rousing the soldiers. But like all men of genius, like all profound men, Claudel was disagreeable. He was disagreeable and incomprehensible. He despised mere elegance, an unpardonable fault in the eyes of Radical party cabinet ministers who had marchionesses as mistresses. Weak characters hate nothing so much as a strong and robust mind. There are things in Claudel that are sublime through their sheer exquisiteness, but Claudel's grace is the grace of a lion and his delicacy is that of the cherubim, or of those bulls with the heads of bearded men. Giraudoux had the irresistible charm of a knowing poodle and he prevailed. Those who mistake elegance for distinction always believe that a poodle clipped in the image of a lion is a real lion. Besides, Claudel was a Catholic poet (as if that still was of the slightest importance). But to the Radicals of 1939 it appeared monstrous.* Poor Giraudoux, to have allowed himself to be clipped in the image of a lion! His pleasant fame can hardly withstand this piece of ridicule.

# XIII

## DISCIPLINE

In the billets of Darius there reigned a spirit of cheerful contentment, thanks to the food, the games of bridge, the sunshine, the general unconcern, plus a little debauchery from time to time. A few old-fashioned, grousing, noncommissioned officers kept on saying that discipline is the chief force of an army, but

* These same curate-baiting Radicals could be seen kneeling at Notre Dame praying God, dear Jesus, and the Virgin Mary for the success of our arms. The front had cracked everywhere, the army was in full flight, but they still hoped for a miracle and went begging God for it. It is hardly possible to imagine anything more dishonorable and more idiotic.

they were hardly listened to. The reserve-force captains, assiduous readers of the *Canard Enchaîné* or the *Oeuvre,* were a little ashamed of these old-fashioned N.C.O.'s. From corporal to colonel, everyone told himself that a soldier in the field is not the same thing as a soldier in barracks, and that men at war must not be annoyed. This reasoning is delightful. I see only one flaw in it: that up to the month of May 1940 the soldiers were not at war. It was therefore indispensable that they *should* be annoyed.

Discipline is as necessary to a soldier as the air he breathes. It is not only the source of his strength, it is also the source of his contentment. The army does away with all individual responsibility and initiative; it allows the soldier not to think. That is the attraction of the army and that explains why so many privates refuse to become officers. An army is a people in good order, and nothing is more soothing than good order; nothing rests the mind so much. In the army, idleness is synonymous with disorder, especially in the French army, where each soldier is longing all the time to become an individual again. War being a state of extreme disorder, it must be met with the most rigorous kind of order. Naturally, the men grumble against discipline, never stop cursing it. I myself found it odious for the short time I was subject to it. But these grumblings are not wholly sincere. Besides, all military duties have a colorful side which makes them something to joke about.

The lieutenants, captains, and colonels in 1940 suffered from the same timidity the cabinet ministers suffered from: they did not dare exercise their authority. It seemed to them that having taken the men away from their work, having put them into uniform, and having sent them to the frontier, there was nothing more they had a right to demand of them. These officers regarded the army as an expression of the French people instead of as an army—that is to say, instead of as a body in absolute submission to a hierarchy, of which every sacrifice can be asked in the name of the nation. But what did they know of the nation, these middle-class, over-clever officers, who in civilian life were engineers or office executives or lawyers? For them war meant being rid of their worries and their wives, leading the life of a pasha with the help of a valet called a batman—a valet, supplied by the State, whom you did not have to pay. Imagine that! How thrilling (and what a windfall) when you have never in your life had anything more than a maid-of-all-work who does not even address you with respect.

# XIV

## *A DOG'S LIFE*

The thing that stands out in my memories of Brittany in 1940 is the sun. The weather was as beautiful as it was in August 1914. I see again the nut trees standing motionless along the unpaved roads which, out of prudence, Cepi made us take. The leaves of the trees seemed polished by the light. The low walls that lined these roads like dams containing streams were so hot that when we sat down on them we scorched our behinds through the thick khaki cloth of our trousers. These elemental, almost animal sensations made a deep impresion. They are indelible in my memory and well up in my mind more strongly than anything else. When I recall those last days of June 1940 the first things that come to my mind are the low walls, the nut trees, and the sun; they have the clarity of a landscape seen only the day before.

In this background I next place the young man I then was, Sergeant Cepi, and my four buddies. After that, it takes a real effort to recall, after fifteen years, the echo of our voices and our broad jokes, the confidences we exchanged, and the songs we sang. Cepi, who had a good build, an attractive mouth, a big nose, and chubby cheeks, told us in detail of all the good luck he had had in his life with the girls. Knowing myself as I do, I must immediately, stung to imitation, have invented similar stories for myself in order to keep up with him.

Tramping across a country that has been turned topsy-turvy, satisfying your needs as you go, catching a glimpse of danger here and there, going where you like and sleeping as you can is a wonderful experience; it is intoxicating; it is living an epic or at least a picaresque novel. For one week we played at being Gil Blas and Ulysses, now looking for adventures and encounters, like a modern hero, now sighing for our homes, like the heroes of old. We appraised events and places with a regal attitude. We saw ourselves as greater than life-size, not realizing that we were actually behaving like romantic Boy Scouts.

Another very sharp memory, or rather a picture, remains with me: we are on a wide, tarred road, a few steps apart from one another. A storm is gathering force—one of those violent, short summer storms—and rain is sweeping the road. Our backs are bent, our overcoats buttoned, our collars turned up, and our steel helmets tilted down over our eyes. I am sure that this picturesque scene, which would have pleased Detaille and Stendhal, gave me intense pleasure at the time. Such scenes can be found on nineteenth-century illustrated plates: pictures of five infantrymen, their rifles covered by their greatcoats, marching along in the rain and mud against the background of a stream and a wall. Beneath is the motto "A Dog's Life." Around the rim of the plate are famous names: Iéna, Friedland, Jemappes, Lodi, Mantua; down the middle are military medals, laurels, shakos and helmets, crossed cannons and ramrods. All this in blue, sepia, red, and black. The memory of that great rain is delicious. I have a number of the same kind of mental snapshots of my life. They don't mean anything very much and they by no means illustrate my happiest or most interesting periods, but as a collection of pictures they are a great success. I have in my head some fifty photographs representing me at all ages and in different surroundings. And in the last resort, this personal album, which I alone can leaf through and where I would look in vain for any outstanding or significant facts, constitutes my most secret and most authentic history. The rest—my successes or misfortunes, the events or works which give me a particular appearance in the eyes of the world—has much less reality.

I did not know, of course, when I was plodding along under the rain in Brittany, that memory was there, like a capricious photographer, registering this moment on its plate. I had plodded under other rains with other companions, and nothing had remained. Poetry always comes without warning. I suppose on that day it had poured in from all quarters: from the east with the Germans, from the south with the heat, from the north with the clouds, from the west with the sea. I suppose it fell from the sky with the rain, rose up from the wet and fragrant earth, and also came forth from my heart. So much poetry could not evaporate entirely. It took on substance; it lodged in a corner of my memory with those other few insignificant and precious moments I had so far experienced, which had escaped in the same way from the daily shipwreck of my feelings, thoughts, and acts. These small things more surely and deeply shape the sensitivity of the mind and give it its own peculiar flavor than any spectacular adventures or tempests of passion.

I did not know that it is sometimes more important to walk for a quarter of an hour under a shower of rain in the month of June than to have killed twenty persons in a memorable battle or seduced the most beautiful woman in France or delivered a fine speech. The laws of the heart are not the laws of morality or history. What remains of a life are a few photographs showing a man with the ten or twelve faces he takes on between birth and death—now standing next to a green plant, now sitting on a Louis Philippe chair. There is nothing to indicate whether this man was chairman of a board of directors, whether his wife was unfaithful to him, or whether he assassinated his father. It is the green plant and the chair, those objects without importance, that will accompany him to the end, to oblivion.

# XV

## *SUMMER MORNINGS*

What is the name of the village where we stopped to get out of the rain? Impossible to remember, any more than I can remember what we did there. I suppose we must have found a friendly welcome, since we did spend the night. Some good soul opened the banqueting chamber of the town hall for us. It was occasionally used for dances. The unwaxed floor smelled of wood—the smell of wood has triumphantly leaped across the fifteen years that separate me from that moment. It was in this fresh and fragrant place, healthy and rustic, that we slept that night. Toward six o'clock in the morning we had a delicious awakening. This often happens when one is twenty, but on this particular morning everything conspired to make it perfect: freedom, our being together, our adventures.

It had gone on raining during the night, and we were a little chilly. But we felt the charm of the summer morning. Outside, the birds were singing; the moisture of the countryside and the lukewarmness of the rising sun came in through the windows. We had slept fully dressed, our heads in our haversacks, having taken off only our boots and our puttees. Walking in stockinged feet on the rough floor of the dance hall, with our shirts hanging out over our trousers, feeling small splinters catching the thick white woolen socks on which our boots had left red stains; a little later singing and stretching ourselves, snorting, with naked bodies under the ice-cold water of a pump—all these are primitive joys rarely experienced again after the age of thirty, joys which in their intensity must resemble those Adam and Eve tasted in the Garden of Eden.

We took to the road again after a Breton breakfast: coffee and milk in a bowl and thick slices of bread covered with half-salty butter. You think you'll never stop eating; it's so good that after the tenth slice you're as hungry as you were in the beginning. The Breton breakfast after the night spent in the banqueting hall was a sensation lying at the juncture of soul and body, just like making love. At twenty, food is the cause of truly metaphysical happiness.

# XVI

## *BURIED*
## *PISTOLS*

After the night spent in the ballroom, Cepi gave up the rather romantic idea of stealing a boat and drifting down the coast to Bordeaux. We had had a lot of fun with the idea for two or three days. The small port we had picked for this act of larceny was called Le Bono. It may even be (I am no longer certain) that it was Le Bono where we slept in the ballroom after the big rainstorm on the road, and where the pretty girl served us with the beef stew I mentioned at the beginning of this story. It would not surprise me. The incomprehensible poetry which descended that day may have welded together the various episodes and set them in my memory. With the passage of time, the episodes have dispersed; the poetic continent has broken up into a number of islands. Each island seems to me now to be a different day, when after all they may be only the scattered fragments of the one day—a day in which my whole journey is summed up.

Not only did it prove impossible to get a boat, but there was no question of doing any fighting. When we reached Le Bono we had already been walking for several days.

The Germans were swarming all over Brittany. At the start we saw only occasional motorcyclists rushing past like arrows and taking possession of the country. The imprint of their tires on the roads seemed to be Hitler's seal, and the whole of France had to be stamped with it as quickly as possible. It was done even before we had realized it.

I have said how we enjoyed our walk across the scenes of the nation's collapse. When we left the ballroom it was already too late to do anything. There were too many Germans everywhere. To fill the cup of our abjection to overflowing, we buried our pistols in a field with the very lively feeling that in doing this we were saving our lives. We felt lighter without our weapons, and that further heightened our gaiety. These pistols were not made for us, fifteen-day-old recruits, peaceful children of Paris, brought up to loathe violence, and used to ease and softness from childhood. Something which always struck me (and which, I must say in justice to myself, I have always detested) was the clinging of the boys of my generation to their childhood and their refusal to leave it. For once, without realizing it, I shared their feelings. I knew how to use a pistol, but a fortnight had not been long enough to get me used to the idea of killing a man, even an enemy. Determination is an acquired state of mind. My comrades had none of it, and neither did I.

As for Cepi, our elder, I cannot really judge him. His life as a traveling salesman, his amorous adventures in trains, his cheap banquets, had ill prepared him for a soldier's trade. He was torn between two duties: patriotism and the safeguarding of his men. It was not really surprising that he chose the second. He was full of the humanitarian and individualistic morality of the thirties. You can justify any system of morality consistently applied, but you cannot justify a mixing of two kinds of morality. France is full of people like Cepi who complain in all good faith about decadence but who practice the indulgent and utilitarian morality of countries which have ceased to believe in their national destiny.

# XVII

## *BOY SCOUTS*

Without our pistols we had irremediably become Boy Scouts. It was no good expecting to escape from enemies who were men and who made no bones about making us see it. Leaving Le Bono with a conquering step we took the direction of Auray. After due thought, Cepi had decided to lead us there.

"I know the town well," he told us. "I spent three months in barracks there and I have friends. We'll be able to see what happens. There are several things we can do. We can get civilian clothes and hide, or my old unit might take us on. At worst we can be taken prisoner. But it doesn't matter very much. France is finished. Peace will be signed in a month and we'll be demobbed."

Here I am obliged to record a rather unpleasant action of Cepi's which at the time seemed wholly admirable to us. We were passing German convoys that hardly spared us a glance. The news was confusing. Was there any fighting still going on anywhere in France? What was England going to do? Cepi, who spoke German, decided simply to ask the *Feldgraus* for the news. Seeing a group of them resting by the roadside, he went up to them, stood to attention in front of an N.C.O., saluted, and said calmly, *"Herr Unteroffizier . . ."* There followed a rather friendly conversation which we didn't understand a word of and the result of which I have forgotten. The *Unteroffizier* was very reserved, and Cepi was all smiles, trying to ingratiate himself. It seems to me that the German was perched on something, a stone or a tank, and that Cepri was humbly raising his head to address him. I noticed vaguely that the difference in their position was somewhat symbolic. But it happens sometimes that one's soul is blinded, and I did not at the time sense the humiliating element in this picture. Like my four buddies, I had jumped to attention too. I was only aware of the superiority of Cepi, who spoke German so well and was not afraid to enter into contact with the enemy. Cepi, by the way, was very conscious of this superiority. He reported to us at great length the news he had extracted from the *Unteroffizier*.

We were determined to reach Auray, where there was a properly constituted unit it would be very comforting to join. We did not even have the daring to consider ourselves "regular deserters," if I may link the two words. Our having kept our uniforms kept us our soldiers' souls, rough and timorous at the same time. They were borrowed souls no doubt, but they completely imprisoned our real souls. A soldier cut off from his regiment, lost in the countryside, is completely confused, because he must make decisions. He hunts for his unit the way an insane man hunts for his will power and his reason.

# XVIII

## *SPECTATOR*

It was between Le Bono and Auray that I became sure of my vocation as an artist—that this vocation was definitely made known to me. After burying my pistol, I walked along for some time in silence. My imagination was conjuring up heroic attitudes for me: leave my buddies, remain alone on the deserted road, and wait behind a heap of leaf-covered stones for the first Germans to show up. There were rifles in the ditches. All I had to do was to pick up one of them and from behind my embattlement shoot until my cartridges were exhausted.* But an insidious voice arose from my heart; it whispered that I ought to stay alive, that I had inestimable work to accomplish, that I knew a small song which nobody could sing in my place. I know that such thoughts invite smiles. I know that nothing is so suspect as this solicitude for yourself, this big price placed on preserving your own existence. But there it is: it is the truth. I experienced this feeling between Le Bono and Auray, and there was nothing about it that resembled an excuse for chicken-heartedness. It was a profound—indeed, I would say an organic—conviction. To go to the root of the matter, I believe I would have been quite content to hide behind a heap of stones and fight to the death; I think I would have done so with enthusiasm. Since I had been walking across Brittany my country had invaded my body through the soles of my boots, so to speak. My feet had taken root in French soil. I had become

---

* What I did not do was done by another artist, the musician Jehan Alain, who, on June 20, 1940, near Saumur, fought singlehanded with his machine gun against a German company until his last cartridge was spent. He was shot after having killed sixteen Germans. The enemy accorded him military honors. (*See* Bernard Gavoty: *Jehan Alain, French Musician*).

French at last, I who had been so certain that I believed in nothing at all and who thought myself so intelligent. Twenty years of a soft and sheltered existence spent reading Anatole France and Mallarmé and remaining ignorant of national and international problems had finally brought me to this state of exaltation, the caricature of which, dating from 1914, had previously seemed so hateful to me.

Seeing the enemy on my soil produced two contradictory feelings in me: a complete detachment on the one hand, and a mad rage on the other, the despair of a man who learns that the woman he loves has given herself to another. It is easy to find fault with this duality, and it would be wrong to see in it, side by side, the artist and the man. They were both there, but not in this clear-cut fashion. They did not constitute such a crude antithesis.

A force which I do not control has always obliged me to remain a spectator, despite myself, in any adventures I have been mixed up in, as though my role were not to act but to observe and afterward retell. Nature places a man where he ought to be and doesn't let him do just anything. My place in the scenes of history is in a corner, apart from what is happening, noting it down on my tablets, in the position of a squatting scribe. One must not force one's talent beyond its natural limits.

# XIX

## *A MAN OF HONOR*

Our attitude toward the peasants was revealing. On the excuse that nothing must be left for the Germans, we assumed that we had a right to everything. We were not far from believing (and in very good faith) that we were unlucky soldiers who had done our full duty. At any rate, without having discussed it at all, we played that part with complete conviction. France, our mother, owed us unconditional aid and protection, and we owed her nothing. We were unfortunate children, prodigal sons. We insisted on fatted calf at each meal, and at six meals a day at that. What was most surprising was that these exorbitant claims were generally accepted. People looked at us with a mixture of fear, compassion, and affection. Our youth and our unconcern moved the civilians to pity: they saw very well that we were only children.

However, I remember one proud peasant who didn't mask his contempt for us. He was the only person during our journey who spoke to us sensibly, in words that had a touch of nobility about them. We had asked him for something or other, a tin of sardines or a loaf of bread. "Get out," he shouted. "If you had fought, you'd be fed now instead of having to beg." We were highly indignant, and this man of honor, the only one we met in a week, narrowly escaped being beaten up. But we were not violent. We swallowed his insults and even managed to find a way of glorifying our patience. "Must try to understand the fellow," Cepi said.

# XX

## *WE DO CARE*

Understand! Understand! For once the word was not used to bury an outrage. But it shocked me, nevertheless. I recognized the fateful word which had poisoned all my childhood, the magic invocation which ruins one's character, the key word of the deplorable French way of education. When I was small and had a quarrel with another boy, a grownup would invariably come along and say, "You are the cleverer of the two; give way." In other words, the function of intelligence is to make capitulation easier. With that kind of reasoning, stupidity always comes out on top. I had more reasoning power at eight than at twenty: this exhortation to the exploited to be "reasonable" always revolted me. I recognized the voice of the grownups as the voice of cowardice. Now that I am a grownup myself, I find myself sick of considering intelligence as an excuse for surrender. The exact opposite is the proper attitude to adopt. On all occasions. Always. Out of respect for truth. I am the more intelligent, *therefore* I am right. And it would be depreciating reason not to ensure its triumph—by force if necessary.

What an extraordinary idea of intelligence has grown up in France. What a disgusting myth it has become. Helmeted Minerva, able to understand the world and strong enough to change it; Minerva, the lean and hardened goddess, the winner of wars, has for us wretched people changed into a stout and languid female, stuffed with sweets and incapable of walking three steps on foot, pleasantly skeptical, and loathing any form of trouble.

This person's power of seduction is incomprehensible. This is the monstrosity, the grotesque idol I meet in the temples of intelligence which are our public administrations, our colleges, and our ministries. If, instead, I were to find there a beautiful young girl, athletic, like the Marseillaise, violent, with eyes flashing like lightning, how I would rush to meet her. But, frankly, this bloated face, this lack-luster look, this paunch filled with the Turkish delight of Anatole France, this painted mouth belching Gidian superficialities into my face, this Radical-

Socialist grandmother disguised as the Princess of Cleves does not attract me.

How can it be explained, this idea of intelligence based on inertia, this enervating doctrine of renunciation, this barroom Buddhism, this resignation of a well-nourished greengrocer who has forgotten that freedom has to be won again every day? Who started it? In what professor's brain of what decadent period was this philosophy born?

I really think it is simply a habit, now sixty or eighty years old, engendered by some republican nonentities who ended up by setting the tone for the whole of the Republic. Every great man, Gambetta, Jules Ferry, Clemenceau, has been tripped up by these smart gentlemen, these realists. The party of inaction invariably grabs hold of the conquests made by the great and squanders them. Its secret is to rule and not to justify itself. And it seems to be a paying proposition. Jules Ferry was thrown out of office for having given France an empire, Léon Blum for having rescued the workers from the *bourgeoisie,* General de Gaulle for having saved our honor and liberated our soil. Moral: Do nothing. Real political wisdom is called Edgar Faure.

To the *Canard Enchaîné,* that flaming torch of intelligence, goes the glory of having proclaimed the motto of present-day France: "What do we care?" These ironical and disillusioned words are spoken with a shrug of

53

the shoulders at the spectacle of the world. They are words of wordly wisdom, a judicious mixture of indulgence and contempt. Without realizing it, the *Canard Enchaîné* discovered the motto of slavery. By repeating and repeating, "What do we care?" we ended up not caring about losing the war, being occupied, dishonored, and trampled on. We "did not care" about the gas chambers and the Buchenwald concentration camp and all the rest. Will the day ever come when instead we shall read in a newspaper and hear shouted by millions of people, "We *do* care!"?

"War is less costly than servitude," said Vauvenargues. An old truth which every event confirms. The choice always is between Verdun and Dachau.

# XXI

## *HELMETS VERSUS TOP HATS*

The cult indulged in for seventy years, the cult of the top hat and adoration of university pedants, ended by leaving its mark on a people. I believe it was around 1885 when the word *intellectual* was first coined and when the conclusion was reached that intelligence was an end in itself and not, as had been thought until then, a means of attaining glory or power. What a wonderful discovery! Intelligence was no longer to be judged by results but by the clothes it wore. The vestments of its high priest were the frock coat, its cross was the umbrella. Happily, Descartes had died two centuries earlier; otherwise it would surely have been proved that for that cavalier to have been a man of gentle birth and a soldier must have spoiled his fine qualities as a mathematician. The effects of this rubbish have been incalculable. The conservatives in France became hostile to intelligence, seeing it in the guise of a Radical party professor, while the left became hostile to force, to struggle, to nature, to reality, and to the nation itself, personified in its eyes by a colonel in an old-fashioned cloak posturing in a drawing room of reactionaries. M. Bergeret versus Gyp! So much mediocrity on both sides drives one to despair.

We are today witnessing the last manifestations of this ridiculous antagonism, the paltry victory of the paltry Bergeret who talks smoothly to us of freedom and justice but who has done everything to disarm France—the source, the mother, and the body of this justice and this freedom. Let France perish rather than that principles should die. But principles do die when their souls die.

# XXII

## IN FRANCE
## ALL EXAMPLES
## ARE WASTED

I can see the reproach that will be leveled at this book. It will be called anarchistic. I by no means accept this label. There is general agreement that when dealing with politics one's choice must be between existing possibilities. Today, this choice means joining a party or subscribing to an ideology. People attach great importance to ideology, so much so that no attention is paid to character. That is what I find hateful. I shall never be able to believe in the superiority of ideas to men. Ideas, like things, are for the service of men. Will power, honesty, morality, a liking for good—these are permanent values without which, in the long run, nothing good is achieved anywhere. Yet they never appear in the speeches of statesmen except as empty phrases or figures of speech. The statesmen only talk of their principles. What a delightful word! As if principles were not what men make them. "Always lean on principles," said Moréas. "They will end by giving way." The joke is profound.

The lack of character in our politicians has, even quite recently, done us great harm. The example of M. Albert Lebrun, last President of the Third Republic, is so striking and shows so well the damage that mediocrity and pusillanimity can cause, that I am astonished nobody has thought of asking what the moral of his example was—not even on the occasion of the obscure death of this former first magistrate of the country. In France today all examples are wasted.

It is a great republican tradition when electing the President to "vote for the stupidest." The politicians are so scared of another *coup d'état* in the style of Napoleon III that they can no longer even imagine electing a man of superior powers to be chief executive. They trust only timidity and stupidity, a disastrous matter since timidity and stupidity always attract far worse calamities than do a spirit of enterprise, firmness of character, and ambition.

Let us suppose for a moment that M. Lebrun had not been either timid or stupid but on the contrary had possessed an ardent heart, a touchy patriotism, a little imagination, and some sense of honor; in short, let us suppose that he had not been *below* the average. What would have happened in 1940?

He would not have resigned, naturally. He would not have handed over power to Pétain, despite the treason, the pressure, and the panic. He would have taken refuge in North Africa. He would have rallied France around his person. He would have preserved the State. Who knows? He might even have taken Pétain with him. All that did not call for any particular intelligence. All it called for was a bit of character. It may even have needed a certain kind of stupidity. But by ill chance the President of the Republic was not afflicted with that special kind of stupidity. The poor man trotted behind the government like an usher. He sobbed nicely over the misfortune of the country. This weak guardian of the constitution could not find the clause that told what a President should do in case of a national disaster. Strong men have within themselves laws (M. Lebrun did not even suspect their existence) and they apply them when no written texts lie to hand. Louis Napoleon was a detestable figure, a real gangster boss. But his seizure of power on December 2, 1851, was less nefarious than M. Lebrun's surrender of power on July 10, 1940, which provided the debasing spectacle of a republic abdicating into the hands of an aged tyrant. Napoleon III at least acted clearly and frankly. In his case one knew what to fight and how to fight it. He seized absolute power by force, and this supposes first of all that there was a plot, something not entirely despicable, something invested even with a certain beauty. But M. Lebrun gave absolute power away for nothing. He brought it on a silver platter to an ancient president-prince bolstered up by the Germans as Thiers had formerly been bolstered up by Bismarck.

As admirable detail: M. Lebrun so pleased the two Houses of Parliament that he was elected President of the Republic a second time in 1939, an honor that until then had fallen only to Jules Grévy, in 1886. Fate apparently doesn't like the powers of French Presidents to be prolonged; it doesn't seem to care for the same transparent characters to be called to office twice in succession. It afflicted the first of these Presidents with a son-in-law who dishonored him. With the second it dealt more severly by precipitating the whole nation into an Aeschylean catastrophe. But isn't it farcical to imagine M. Lebrun in the role of Prometheus? The idea of M. Lebrun chained to the Caucasus for having stolen a spark of divine lightning for the benefit of France conjures up a picture that will amuse those who knew this excellent man. Supposing Jupiter had indeed wanted to chastise him: he would have been forced to look for him with a magnifying glass in the depths of his little Élysée Palace. Ought I to say that people have the Prometheuses they deserve? No doubt they do. But nothing is ever lost for good, and six months are enough to change the face of the world. Dame Fortune is a good sport: given the smallest encouragement, a semblance of good will, a slightly generous idea, a young man with a little spirit, or the beginning of a popular movement, she will come back with rushing wings. Only a vacuum disgusts her. The past ten years have made the French people sensitive; they have their

ears close to the ground. The first tremor, however slight, will be picked up at once and Dame
Fortune, whose ear is more finely attuned still,
will hear it, however far away she is hiding.

# XXIII

## *THE MAN*
## *OF*
## *DESTINY*

The career of M. Albert
Lebrun until his first election as President of the
Republic is little known. Still, people do remember that he was the head of his year at the École
Polytechnique. He was therefore a brilliant stu-
dent. But this career, which started with so much
promise and ended in capitulation, is very instructive. The École Polytechnique taught its star
pupil ballistics and integral calculus. But it did
not teach him to steel his soul against adversity.
And this was the school in about 1900, when it
was worth a hundred times what it is worth today.
God knows, I've mocked often enough at the word
faith and whatever object it was applied to (and
I was not wrong, for all the faiths proposed to
me wearied me: the faith of Péguy, the faith of

the vicar of Saint Ferdinand, the faith of Barrès, the faith of Poincaré, the faith of Hitler, the faith of Thorez, and plain faith most of all because that is simply a word), but what I overlooked was that M. Lebrun did not have any faith either. No professor had been present to give this excellent pupil a course in faith. Faith was not inscribed in the curriculum of the Polytechnique. There was no written or oral examination on the subject when leaving the school. How it is that until I was twenty-two or twenty-three, when I understood it by myself, nobody told me that faith was synonymous with passion, and great passion at that? And that without passion (preferably great) a man is insipid? That is a truth which would have moved me and saved me a lot of time. Is faith then the prerogative of duffers only? (I mean intelligent duffers who read good authors in secret.) Now that I am grown up and see a few small things that did not strike me fifteen years ago, it is people without faith who weary me. I find them dull and ineffective. Above me, I find them far removed from essentials. The "men of little faith" who are denounced from time to time are not the aggressive men; they are the lukewarm men, the Laodiceans, those whom the École Polytechnique taught how to fire a cannon but not that the cannon was to be pointed at the enemy. For if it is futile to oppose ideas with bullets, it is more futile still to answer bullets with philosophical speeches. A community in which the duffers are in fact right and the good pupils wrong is in serious need of an over-hauling.

It is customary to call the great figures who change the course of history "men of destiny." I believe that is the name Victor Hugo gave to Napoleon. For our twentieth-century France the man of destiny was called Albert Lebrun. Who would have believed it in 1937, when the music-hall singers were composing songs about his big feet and his tendency to weep on every occasion?

Albert Lebrun stood at the parting of the ways between a powerful France and a France fallen into decay. He opened the trap door of the dungeon into which France fell. This small gesture, a hand on a lever and a raised flag, had vaster consequences than fifteen years of victorious campaigns and that heroic period which, a century and a half later, is still celebrated every day by historians and poets. We needed an Achilles. We got a Thersites, and a melancholy Thersites at that, incapable even of making a small joke we might have laughed at.

# XXIV

## *CASSANDRA*
## *AT THE*
## *HELM*

One is dumfounded by the optimism that determines every act and every text of our governments. After all, we have had other national disasters in our history. How is it then that no constitutional document lays down in detail what must be done when the country is invaded by an enemy,* when the government is dispersed, or when the nation is enslaved?

These are burning problems which could arise again one of these days. Nothing happens in the French Republic except in terms of a precedent. Does this mean that next time we shall have the Vichy buffoonery all over again and that the Pétain, or rather the Lebrun, precedent will have force of law? If we refuse to foresee the worst—that is, a France completely Polandized, partioned between Great Russia and Great America—we can be sure that the worst will happen. I want statesmen

* It was not always so. For example, Article 4 of Chapter XXV of the Constitution of 1793 states: "The French people do not make peace with an enemy who occupies its territory." Short but unambiguous.

who are somber and uneasy and who do not hide their cast of mind. I want a Cassandra Cabinet. I want to see Cassandra in power wearing her black veils; for I believe—in fact I am certain—that only Cassandra, keeping permanently before our eyes the specter of catastrophe, can lead us toward a renewal of our power. When one is most unhappy one must be most pessimistic. There is no other way of salvation. One can only allow oneself a small touch of optimism when one is at the summit of happiness and glory, and even that is very dangerous. Optimism is what the Greeks called *hubris*, a boasting, a lack of proportion. Nothing irritates the Gods more. But pessimism is modesty itself. Modesty alone leads on to shining fortune and preserves it. When one acts all the time as if death were about to overtake one tomorrow, one has unlimited power, the invincible and indifferent power of desperation.

There are circumstances in which it is Cassandra's turn to speak. But weak governments set up a rival to interrupt her. This rival is the censorship. What an edifying essay could be written under the title "Cassandra and Anastasia," a fine historical review going back to the war of Troy. Alas, it was the Trojans, about to be vanquished, to whom Cassandra addressed the dark prophecies that were not listened to. Is there a finer spectacle than Winston Churchill gravely and without prevarication speaking in the House of Commons on the appalling state of England in June 1940 and announcing the trials to come? ". . . We shall not flag or fail. . . . We shall defend our island, whatever the cost may be. We shall fight on the beaches. . . . We shall fight in the fields and in the streets.*. . . We shall never surrender." Brave and virile words. A country that could say them and could listen to them deserved to win.

I have always hated optimism. It seems to me to be the most characteristic expression of a weak mind (only optimists commit suicide). In a government the offense is doubled because it is an insult to the people. Official optimism has nothing in common with the exaltation generated by a great policy or by acts of daring. It is a state of mind governments encourage in order to be able to carry on with the stupidities they have already initiated. "Tell the nation the truth." This little sentence has terrified every cabinet minister for the past thirty years. These dear ministers are sick-nurses: they are perpetually trying to comfort with artificial smiles and white lies. France is so old, so capricious, so impotent. She must be handled gently, the dear senile thing. You couldn't think of telling her brutally that she is suffering from cancer or that she must have a leg cut off. She could never stand it. Let's wait for the leg to rot and fall off by itself. It will hurt less that way.

* At this point, it seems, Churchill put his hand over the microphone and said, in an aside, "And we will club them with beer bottles, for that is about all we've got."

# XXV

## *SLEEP WALKING*

Last year * at a public
meeting I heard a really crushing remark: that
the French Parliament represents the country perfectly and that our politics are exactly what we
want them to be. Such an assertion is too revolt-
ing to be immediately accepted. It is nevertheless
true. There is always between the government
and the nation a kind of collusion over and above
political programs and conflicting ideas. It is a
sentimental collusion. We know each other so well
that there is no need to say anything, and with
marvelous tact cabinet ministers sense the secret
mind of the country that has carried them to
power. In decadent democracies subtle and decisive communications are exchanged between the
nation and the government: mediocrity outbids
itself. Since France ceased to hanker after glory,
what a paradise the country has become for second-
rate politicians. How can ministers still be afraid of
this docile and inert nation, of this people of slaves
who put up with every injustice. Yet they dare
not move; they might wake the country. France
is going through a period of sleepwalking. I mean
the France of today, which is not the France of

* Written in 1956.

the past or, I hope, the France of the future. I am reminded of Miguel de Unamuno, who started a lecture with the words *"España, mi madre . . . no, España mi hija,"* and thus showed that he was not talking to the feeble and stupid Spain which was preparing to become the old mistress of a bandit, but to the Spain of tomorrow, the daughter of his teaching, for which we are still waiting, in which Lorca will at last be reunited with Cervantes and where at last the people will have relearned what life is.

"France, my mother . . . no, France my daughter," I often say to myself with a little happiness, a little despair, a little tenderness. Nothing is predestined. It only requires love and genius to turn an old witch who is thinking of retiring and quietly dying into a marvelous adolescent. But where is this love? Where is this genius?

# XXVI

## *THE GALLIC COCK ON THE SPIT*

At certain unfortunate periods of history the Gallic temperament seems to have lost all its virtues and kept only its vices.

We are unfortunately living in one of those periods now, and it makes one long to damn this temperament to hell. For it is this temperament, quick to become discouraged, prompt to become violent, enflamed by chimeras, living on mirages, disorderly and stupidly brave, that is the cause of all our defeats.

Is there a more ridiculous bird than that which King Louis Philippe plucked as an emblem for us from the flagpoles of the Revolution? The cock! That vain and noisy fowl, ludicrously amorous, both timid and foolhardy, unequaled in stupidity—that barnyard dandy, that feathered pimp! Natural history is not lacking in powerful or dignified animals without our having had to go looking for this candidate for the stew pot. Personified by such a creature, how can we be anything but a subject for mockery to the rest of Europe. Under Louis XIV, the Frenchman was majestic and a person to be feared. The musician of the eighteenth century wrote compositions "in the French taste" which are surprising in their gravity. Today, outside our frontiers, something quite different is understood by "French taste." From being majestic, we have become ridiculous. As for the Gallic cock, its beak gaping, its feathers bristling, and its image cast in brass on the top of innumerable monuments to the dead of the war of 1914, it perfectly symbolizes our swashbuckling governments busy burying us to the sound of joyful cock-a-doodle-doos. We have shifted from the eagle to the cock. The last stage is that of the ostrich hiding its head in the sand while someone plucks the feathers from its behind. Perhaps a new Louis Philippe will dare to endow us with this hitherto unused emblem and thereby complete the cycle. After all, there is an element of greatness in dying in abjection. This aged and flouted France, once so noble and so powerful, reminds me of Don Rodríguez, the hero of Claudel's *The Satin Slipper,* dying in misery after having been viceroy of America. An ignominious death is the fate of the very greatest men, and of the truest.

The "myth of the glorious defeat," which I have mentioned earlier, is a favorite subject for the songs of the cock. The Gallic temperament, in fact, admires the gesture more than the result, perceives glory more clearly than profit, and discerns false glory better than real achievement and true honor. This myth, so deadly when it gets a hold on a nation, presides over our history * as reconstituted by the Third Republic. The first French national hero is Vercingetorix, a defeated chieftain, more celebrated and popular than Richelieu just because of his defeat, his steadfastness in adversity, and his tragically heroic end, in which not even humiliation was lacking. Up to this point, there is nothing reprehensible in the cult. The confusion comes

* It presides also over the history of our literature with the *Chanson de Roland.* School textbooks are entitled "From the *Chanson de Roland* to Our Own Day."

later. In time all the acts of Vercingetorix were magnified. Admiration for what was admirable spread to what was not—to the lack of preparation and lack of discipline of the "Gallic army," to the shortsighted views of its general, and to the disorder and inexperience that permitted so much bravery and unleashed much gallantry. What prodigies of valor the soldiers of Gaul displayed against Caesar. Ah, the insolent nation! The Gauls were perhaps a hundred times braver than the Romans in the Gallic wars, but it is the Romans who won and the Roman Empire that led the world. The Gauls consoled themselves with their useless (and costly) bravery.

There is in Gaul a kind of "intoxication of despair," a very peculiar thing, because it exists together with a great deal of energy and a strong desire to live. It is what later was named *panache*. This detestable panache, this posy of white feathers, was graceful on the bonnet of Henry IV and waved bravely in the wind at the battle of Ivry. But it has developed in the course of the centuries into an extravagant monument of futility. This bunch of feathers has become a huge cloud of smoke covering the whole of France and blinding her. France no longer sees anything more than the fanciful figures this deceptive smoke screen conjures up before her eyes.

# XXVII

## *FRENCH CANNIBALS*

Mention of the word *panache* brings visions of the French nobility before the French Revolution. But what do people really know about this nobility? Montmorency-Boutteville, who had his head cut off for dueling, was a pretty savage fellow who had on his conscience the lives of a handful of undistinguished citizens about as worthless as himself. He was violent and haughty, and his nobility bore no resemblance to the dreamy or jingoistic foolishness which was made fashionable by the Romantic movement and which Rostand, that singer of the French middle classes, made ridiculous once and for all. Or again, take Cinq-Mars, who is usually represented, on the covers of some of Alfred de Vigny's books, as a young man with girlish features and a fine mustache. The true description of him written by Tallemant des Réaux shows him to have been a third-rate intriguer, a dolt who kept his position only because of the special taste Louis XIII had for him.

It is interesting to know at what period the word *panache* was first coined, in its sense of spectacular and more or less gratuitous deeds of valor. Littré's dictionary does not mention it. *Panache* in the above sense seems to have sprung up toward the end of the last century. From the fourteenth to the eighteenth century the word meant only "bundle of feathers or other light objects which, being tied at the bottom and fluttering at the top, form a kind of posy." The panache fixed to the hat or helmet was a sign of nobility. It is nevertheless rather more than just a coat of arms or a sign of recognition: it is a mark of ridicule. Mathurin Régnier and Boileau, better poets than Rostand, who also had the advantage over him of having lived at the period of this famous panache, never mention it except to make fun of it. It is obvious that what gave France her greatness between 1515 and 1815 was not the showing off of a few chicken-brained swashbucklers waving feathers about all over the place. The opposite is true: France built her greatness by fighting unremittingly against the panache tendency in her national temperament.

General Lassalle, killed at Wagram, used to smoke a pipe when leading his cavalry charges. There is a picture of him doing so in the Army Museum in Paris. It was painted by Édouard Detaille, a painter of military subjects, who was devoid of imagination and who would never have invented a pleasing detail of this kind. Lassalle is untidily dressed, there is a smile on his face, and instead of a sword he is brandishing a Gambier pipe (or perhaps it was a Scouflaire). His horse is galloping. A few yards behind him come the hussars shouting red

72

Indian war cries in a tremendous clanking of arms and a tumult of hoofs, neighings, and horses' farts, their swords pointed forward and their carbines at the saddlebow. A bugler is blowing away for dear life, the solo performer in this concerto of guns and shouts.

What Detaille, who is the Rostand of painters, has failed to render is the soul of General Lassalle, the soul his real smile would have expressed if he had really smiled at that moment. He had the soul of a cannibal and his smile was terrible.

# XXVIII

## *MIXING MORALITIES*

Every soldier, every general, has the soul of a red Indian chief, a fact completely missed by the second-rate writers who manufacture panache after the event and by the young idealists of Saint-Cyr who read these authors and then go into battle wearing white gloves. The white gloves are admirable, and I am glad they were worn by French hands. But if I had been the colonel in charge, I would have forbidden the wearing of white gloves on pain of confinement to barracks. It should be remembered that war in lace (the phrase was coined by Georges d'Esparbès, a journalist on the newspaper *Gaulois* around 1900), which delights so many sensitive persons, blossomed out during the reign of Louis XV, a disastrous reign for France.

I must confess that I have always felt a deep-seated aversion to M. d'Auteroche, who told the English at the battle of Fontenoy, "You shoot first." This seems to me an expression of the maddest sort of vanity. M. d'Auteroche had no right to sacrifice the safety of his country and the lives of his soldiers to his blustering foolhardiness. If Louis XV had had a bit of common sense, he would have had this M. d'Auteroche shot for his untimely gentleman-liness. But Louis XV himself presented an example of the worst type of panache when he declared at the end of the war of the Austrian succession, "The King of France is not a merchant," which was an insult to the privations his people had suffered during the war.

Here one gets to grips with the fundamental vice in this panache, with the irreducible contradiction the attitude implies: the incompatibility I denounced earlier as "mixing two kinds of morality." The panache spirit is the application to collective actions of rules of morality made for the individual. But collective actions are governed by their own system of ethics, by the morality of nations. That the Count d'Auteroche wished to die in a knightly manner is altogether charming, but it was his private business. In inviting our good soldiers and the kingdom of France to commit suicide with him, he was singularly overstepping his functions. He had forgotten, if he ever knew, that duty calls upon a man to die for his country in case of absolute need, as did that authentic hero, the Chevalier d'Assas, but that until the imperative moment arrives he should live for the good of the service.

As for Louis XV's refusing to extract every ounce of advantage for France from the Treaty of Aix-la-Chapelle, in the name of Heaven knows what delicate feelings (which must have vastly amused the great Frederick), at best he behaved like a gentleman. He decidedly did not behave like a king.* In his memoirs Duguay-Trouin, the illustrous admiral of Louis XIV, who was a real warrior and a great man and who had nothing in common with the laced fools of his time, put things back in their proper perspective. He was talking with the Count of Innsbruck about the motives which

* Yet to us today this mediocre Louis XV, who is accused in the history textbooks of having sold Canada, seems worthy of some admiration. It is forgotten that he was dealing with the Canada of the eighteenth century and not with the Canada of today, with "the few acres of snow" mentioned by Voltaire (who was no stupider than a history professor of the Fourth Republic). The men who lost Indo-China, sold off Morocco, and gave up the Indian settlements from *weakness,* not from generosity, have no right to upbraid Louis XV for having sold a few acres of snow. At least he got something for them.

drive nations to make war on one another. The count remarked, "The French fight for booty, the Germans fight only for glory." To which M. Duguay replied coldly, "Yes, each of us fights for what he has not got."

# XXIX

## "VIEILLE FRANCE"

The enemies of the Republic hardly remember what the France of 1788, the France of lace cuffs and exquisite manners, was like. The current political polemicists who name their paper *Rivarol* should read Rivarol's political reflections. Although he was a Royalist, he cast a cold eye at his own party. Rivarol's thinking has the splendid lucidity which lost causes inspire in people who are worth more than the causes they espouse. A hundred and sixty years later his meditations on the dying monarchy and its European allies apply word for word to our middle-class democracy. I cannot resist quoting the most characteristic of his sayings relating to the condition of the *émigrés* and their foreign allies: "They are always late by a year, by an army, and by an idea."

Whenever anybody mentions *"Vieille* France," it is always with admiration in his voice. It is synonymous with the aristocratic regime and its grand manners. Yet what an accusation the alliance of those two words *Ancient France* contains. The France of 1788 was old indeed—very old, even decrepit. She had all the vices of old age: frivolity, futility, debility, and, if you look more closely, stupidity. She was not the France of the philosophers, of Rousseau and Diderot, but an old, capricious, obscurantist, and timorous power, vacillating in its governing between flabbiness and harshness. People often speak of the "gang of mediocrities" who block the road for men of capacity and who will forgive everything except talent. I assume this gang held all the posts under Louis XVI, as it does today.

Carrying the thing to such lengths should cause alarm, for mediocrity bears within itself the seeds of its own death and looks on with indifference at the catastrophes it produces, giving no thought to the final catastrophe by which it will be engulfed. The Revolution of 1789 and the Terror were solemn warnings: it was not so much the aristocrats whose heads were being cut off; it was stupidity which was being decapitated. Rivarol reveals himself as undoubtedly the best analyst of that period when he writes: "To make a revolution you have greater need of a certain mass of stupidity on one side than a certain dose of light on the other." The mass of stupidity which made the French

Revolution was produced by the court. In comparison, the weak dose of light produced by the speeches of Vergniaud shone out like a beacon. The Russian Revolution of October 1917 was produced by the profound idiocy reigning at the court of Nicholas II. Republican and democratic France in 1956 has almost, if not wholly, attained the degrees of stupidity of the monarchist France of 1788 and of Imperial Russia of 1916. One more sentence from Rivarol in order to finish with all this. He said of the nobles: "They mistook their memories for rights." This remark applies to all Frenchmen today.

# XXX

## *THE ARMY*
## *OF*
## *MEMORY*

Rivarol's remark already applied to the French in 1925, but they had not yet realized it. The French army of 1940 was nothing but a great memory, a mist that disappeared as soon as it was blown upon. I myself saw this phantom fade away and vanish. It was a thing without a body and without a soul, a sort of undulating ectoplasm cast lightly over the land of our fathers, a veil, a vapor of men.

I found the French army at Auray. When we got there—Cepi, my buddies and myself—there were several thousand men waiting placidly in a sort of happy dejection for someone to take away from them the unlovely khaki-colored uniforms with which they had been afflicted for ten months. These soldiers at last took up the silent-role for which they felt they had been born. For you don't say a word and you don't move when you mistake your memories for rights. Except for the color, the khaki uniform of 1940 was the same as the light blue in 1914. The steel helmet, with its badge in the shape of a grenade and its raised ridge intended to blunt strokes from a sword, was the same the 1914 poilus had worn. To increase the resemblance many men had let their beards grow. If you screwed up your eyes and forgot the excremental color, you could believe you were back twenty-five years. And, good Heaven, I am forgetting the greatcoat, the famous, glorious trenchcoat turned up at the bottom and buttoned in the style of Louis XVIII. I am also forgetting the rifles, complete with their long bayonets. But I have good reason for forgetting the rifles: when I got to Auray they had been surrendered a long time before and piled up in storerooms by the conquerors. From the end of June 1940 the French army appeared to me to be an army of memory, a herd of supers bunched together at the back of the

79

stage, dressed in costumes copied from the cast-off clothes of past periods of history. They were the halberdiers of *Faust* singing "Immortal Glory to Our Ancestors." Poor halberdiers, who for a brief moment had dared come to the front of the stage and who were promptly sent back to the wings.

What part did this army take in the drama of the war? The worst part possible. It believed that it was enough for it to show itself, that it was entitled merely be showing itself to carry off the victory, that Memory was a faithful and all-powerful god, that the words *France* and *French army* were magic more murderous than cannon and machine guns, more powerful than virtue. I heard one of those defeated soldiers, caught at Auray like a rabbit in a trap, repeating with complete conviction a remark I had often heard in my childhood, which was no longer true: "There are only two kinds of good soldier in the world: the French and the German." Did he believe the outworn phrase, this prisoner, this coward? Yes, he probably did. He too was living in his memories. A minimum of honesty obliged him to mention the Germans, a month earlier he might not even have done that.

# XXXI

## *A FEMALE NATION*

The war of 1914 has been called the war of right because we won it. That alone showed that right has to be won, and at the cost of some effort; that it has to be won all the time. Rights do not long outlive the strength employed to defend them. Our war of 1939–1940 was the War of Memory. I can find no other name for this desperate enterprise supported by neither faith nor courage. The French let themselves drift into the war by sheer routine —simply doing what they had done before. When you begin a war as supernumeraries, you finish it as slaves. A man who does not act is a thing, and it is right that he should be treated as such— that is to say, that he should be made a slave. In 1940, everything happened as if France were going forward as a body to offer herself to the Germans. The Germans took hold of a million and a half sheep, and their work was limited to herding them somewhere. If one thinks of the part played later in French life by the prisoners of war, of the importance attached to them, of the solicitude and the lyricism they inspired, and of the legend that grew up about them, one is bound to agree that the vocation of this army was not battle but captivity.

The French soldiers the Germans locked up after a month of fighting and flight became highly romantic persons. They were Saint Louis, prisoner of the Saracens, or Francis I, captive in Spain, reproduced a million and a half times. They were clad in the romantic aura of the man detained far from home against his will and dying of homesickness. France was at a loss to know how to raise the ransom for these princes who had lost everything (including their honor). With the passing of time aberrations of the moral sense can be measured. A hundred years from now, if the world survives so long, people will have difficulty conceiving that it was seriously proposed to have prisoners of war released in exchange for civilians—in other words, to let the innocent take the place of the guilty. There was no gold with which to pay the ransom, and there has never been any substitute for gold other than blood. The movement of pity in France for the prisoners is symptomatic: it is a feminine reaction, the reaction of a mother who has only tenderness and mercy to offer her unworthy sons. Here again we see two distinct systems of morality being confused. Meekness and leniency are sentiments that honor the individual but condemn a nation to death. To forgive offenses and love those who harm him, to save them at the cost of his own safety, may raise a man to the level of a saint but drag down a country to the abject rank of a female nation.

# XXXII

## *MIXING MORALITIES* (2)

Duty is never simple, never easy, and rarely obvious. A nation that replaces contempt with love is failing in its duty (and incidentally does not have to wait long to be punished). It is being untrue to the morality proper to its own nature, to principles which have been laid down for thousands of years and gathered together as "reasons of State." These celebrated reasons of State call for imposture, perjury, injustice, crime, and the sacrifice of innocents in the name of a political abstraction. These reasons of State, hateful and derided as they are, are as necessary to the life of a country, and indeed to the whole of mankind, as courage is for the safekeeping of a warrior. As long as France believed in her reasons of State, as long as she sensed them and lived them—if need be in pain— she remained a virile nation. If she wants to become so again, she must once more believe in the reasons of State, and her thinkers, cabinet ministers, journalists, soldiers, and indeed the whole people must at last give up the baleful habit of practicing day in and day out two incompatible acts of moral principles. The so-called committed writers, who have been running about in great numbers of recent years, furnish a good example of this confusion of two distinct moralities, for they obstinately go on applying the criteria of individual ethics to collective actions or actions accomplished in the name of a collectivity. We see the denouncing in many articles and booklets events that revolt their kindly hearts. This indignation, it seems, greatly stirs public opinion. Yet their indignation has little more influence than the armchair strategy of bar loungers or the plans of family men who begin their remarks with, "Now, if I were the government . . ."

It is odd that nobody seems to realize the folly of this pompous lack of understanding. The opinion of Chateaubriand matters a great deal, but not the slightest importance attaches to the ideas of a hundred or so pleasant young men who may possibly have published a novel about love or a volume of indifferent poems. I do not believe they express the voice of "the universal conscience." Anatole France held that the universal conscience did not exist (which showed he was a poor Socialist). It does exist, but it is not made up of the sum of individual consciences. It is far more subtle than that and far more disconcerting: the universal conscience belongs to the same nature of things as do reasons of State.

I blush to recall this old-established truth, which has been obvious through the centuries and which was developed a hundred times under Louis XIV: that kings cannot look at things with the eyes of private citizens. To try to force them to do so is cruel folly: it is forcing down to the level of detail a mind whose duty it is to look at things from on high. This reasoning does not lead to oppression and violence; it does not excuse badly conducted wars or the excesses of the police or of bad colonists. It aims only at destroying the modern error of reducing problems of government to attitudes of sentimentality.

I am certainly not the first person to say this, but it cannot be repeated too often—that nothing is less effective and more deadly than the sniveling humanitarianism of the Moderate Left. (The Extreme Left believes in reasons of State as much as Cardinal Richelieu did and chastely closes its eyes to their savage necessities.) Honesty, justice, humanity, mercy, self-respect, and respect for others are not irreconcilable with reasons of State: only a little skill and character are called for. History provides several examples, among others that of Saint Louis, a great saint and a great leader of men— and in addition a Frenchman, a coincidence which, we confess, gives us some pleasure.*

* With regard to a small police problem, it is quite stimulating to compare the doctrine of Saint Louis with that of the Popular Republican Movement (the Catholic party) today. Saint Louis opened the brothels, the Catholic party closed them. Saint Louis did not confuse the morality of the State with the morality of the individual. The Popular Republican Movement does.

# XXXIII

## *DISORDER*

The beginning of my captivity at Auray comes back to me as a rather pleasant time—more agreeable in any case than the week which had just gone by, whatever enjoyment the six of us may have had from our walk. Actually, eight days had been enough to exhaust our desire for freedom and our taste for the unexpected. We had had enough walking and enough living like adventurers. We longed to throw off our burdens. To be responsible for ourselves was too much. We wanted to place ourselves as quickly as possible in the hands of a chief, French for preference, but a German would do. We were inferior minds, and it is curious to note the feeling of guilt such minds have as soon as they are left to themselves and forced to act on their own initiative. They believe they are usurping a part, and this makes them uncomfortable; they are afraid all the time of putting their foot in it. Eight days had been enough to make our dangerous and unwarranted independence a burden to us.

I have mentioned the lightheartedness engendered in us by the disorder into which France had been plunged; but this disorder was too different from what we had been used to for it to offer any real attraction for very long. The intoxication of walking straight ahead without any sort of obstacle across a community turned topsy-turvy and in a country stripped bare of any administrative civilization, where everything was allowed since nothing was any longer forbidden, soon gave way to a feeling of embarrassment.

The countryside in Brittany had offered a complete picture of a lawless world. German regiments were going by in all directions (as a matter of fact, they were heading for the sea, but we who saw them everywhere did not understand this); French soldiers in disorderly retreat passed one another in opposite directions; the peasants, with anxious faces, were expecting to be looted. When we left our camp we looted a bit ourselves. We had been taught to respect military equipment more than our own lives, but from one day to the next it suddenly ceased to have the slightest value. Before ordering us to retreat, or rather before throwing the doors open to the stampede, officers and noncommissioned officers had half ordered us to carry away as much equipment as we could. I remember I chose a magnificent cavalry greatcoat, several blankets which I rolled into the shape of a sausage, haversacks, water bottles, and even, God forgive me, a pair of binoculars. All these things had been reposing peacefully and neatly in the camp store. The look of the store after we left was well calculated to provoke reflections on the misfortunes of being defeated. The whole camp, which we were the last to leave and which only the day before had looked as clean and neat as a new pin, with its trim little huts and stiff tents, was now a scene of desolation. It looked like an oasis put to the sack by a band of Bedouin robbers.

# XXXIV

## *DISORDER* (2)

When Paris was being liberated in 1944, I had a wonderful experience: I saw the entire nation spontaneously abolish private property and pool all its resources. If anybody were asked for anything, twenty people were immediately ready to provide it, whether it was a piece of bread or an automobile. There were in this mutual aid and this temporary sharing of one's possesions a joy and a generosity which I am glad to have known once in my life, and particularly in this country. I was a fighting man— at least I had again become a fighting man. I took part in the skirmishes which broke out at certain points in Paris. They weren't very important, probably, but there was a lot of firing and it was sometimes very murderous. I felt I was the son of all Parisians. I was back in the bosom of my family—a family delightfully united, a tough and courageous family of people reconquering their freedom. I was among men and not among sheep. There were no longer any unknown persons. Everyone I met in the streets, soldiers or onlookers, wore the same warm smile: the old people offered their possessions, the young offered their lives.

Nowadays there is not much opportunity to talk about these things (and, besides, there is hardly any inclination to do so), and I am glad to be able to say in passing that this week of the nineteenth to the twenty-sixth of August, 1944, was one of the best periods of my life, that these seven days consoled me for four years of anxiety and boredom and for the sadness in which the collapse of 1940 had left me, without my being fully conscious of it. During the liberation of Paris I noticed as great a disorder as that in Brittany four years earlier, but it was of an absolutely different kind. It was a joyful disorder, a fruitful disorder, the disorder of war—of a successful war, not of a rout. Out of this disorder a new state was going to be born. We were preparing the way for General de Gaulle, who was coming back to us from England with our honor, the honor which all alone he had carried away with him, which he had not found too heavy to bear, which he had preserved intact, and which he was bringing back to us to decorate our new escutcheon with.

# XXXV

## *DISORDER* *(3)*

The disorder in Brittany in 1940 was ominous. It was the disorder that precedes death. People did not give then with joy but with despair in their hearts. They gave as a dying man distributes what he owns. They gave us wine to drink and food to eat without asking for money. They gave us shoes and opened their barns for us, saying to themselves that since all was lost anyhow it was better to let us have it than the Germans. We soldiers, as I have already said, very easily adapted ourselves to that state of mind, and after two days we had raised it to the level of a philosophy. Having had everything given to us the first day, we concluded next day that everything was due us, and after that we discovered very well how to ask for it. In lost countries one behaves as in conquered countries—even more harshly, for the conqueror usually hopes to live a long time on the land he has invaded and believes that it is in his own interest to show some consideration. But the vanquished have no concern for the soil they have deserted; on the contrary, they ruin it as much as they can; they carry off what can be borne away and break up the rest. They do it partly from rage at being forced to abandon it, the way a woman hurls vitriol into the face of the man who has thrown her over; they do it partly from calculation: the enemy must find no resources. Scorched earth is hardly a form of tactics; it is a reaction of passion, of despair. Cepi, my four buddies, and I applied it unconsciously, within the limits of our powers. We snatched a chicken here, stole a shirt there, and so on. These small, shabby thefts were appropriate to our defeat. We needed a Souvaroff. All we had was Pétain. It was up to the army to instigate a scorched-earth policy. Since we had not been able to defend our country, we were no longer under any obligation to respect it. We should have gone on to the bitter end and reclaimed ourselves by killing our country rather than leaving in it the smallest trace of beauty for the benefit of the conqueror. But the High Command, which had failed in its own duty once, did not consider it had the right to start fulfilling its duty then. Who, anyhow, would have listened to this infirm and timorous Command? One is prepared to sacrifice oneself for a man in whom one has some confidence but not for some poor creature without power of decision and without strength. Besides, what an inhuman thing it would have been to set fire to a France so gentle and so lovely! The French were too much in love with their own landscapes. Even in these most desperate straits, when an implacable enemy had robbed them not only of their freedom but of the refined setting of their existence, the French still hoped for a miracle, they still believed that one day someone would hand them back their country and the taste for living in it.*

The miracle happened: the taxis of the Marne this time were the ships of D-Day, but the miracle was incomplete. France was handed back to us but not the taste for living in it. The men who are modeling the face of France today are the same men who lost the war of 1940. There is an element of baseness in being happy today in France, a prosperous country where there is plenty to eat, where there is much to enjoy. Material welfare is not a negligible quantity, of course, but it is secondary. And the fact that at present it is being made the sole aim of national ambition shows cruelly that we are living in one of the saddest periods of our history. For we have all the food we need, a great many automobiles, and very little popular revolt. (Are the people satisfied or are they just dejected?) In short, we are living among the material comforts of a great nation but we have no honor. We really didn't care about that frail honor which was miraculously preserved and brought back to us from London by General de Gaulle.

Do not take the sentence that follows as an appeal for a dictator or an expression of regret that there isn't one, but simply

* The defeat of 1871 was less serious than that of 1940: it was a complete defeat and thus closed the door to any miracle. There was nothing to count upon except energy and rage and saving money in order to pay the five milliard francs of reparations to liberate the occupied provinces.

as what I feel in the most sensitive region of my heart—the place where, as everyone knows, the love of one's country resides: I believe that French honor has followed General de Gaulle into retirement.

# PART TWO

## The Victim Cast for the Leading Part

IT IS A TERRIBLE ADVANTAGE TO HAVE DONE
NOTHING, BUT IT MUST NOT BE CARRIED TOO FAR.

—Rivarol

# I

## *CAVALRYMEN*
## *WITHOUT*
## *HORSES*

I wish I could recall our feelings when, after our week on foot, we caught sight of the town of Auray; but I cannot. I hardly even remember the town. Yet all that should have remained engraved on my heart, if only because it was so picturesque. To arrive on foot in a town held by the enemy is an adventure worthy of the Middle Ages. It suggests some revolutionary epoch before the invention of automobiles and airplanes, when humanity was still dominated by the great civilization of the horse: a period which lasted until the twentieth century and is already entirely forgotten.

We must have halted outside the town, as the pilgrims of Péguy did when they first caught sight of the cathedral of Chartres, that thin straight column of smoke rising from the plains of Beauce; as defeated soldiers—irregulars in rags, flea-bitten legionnaires, or horseless cavalrymen—have done since the beginning of history when reaching the end of their flight. Haven and prison, Auray marked the end of our mean little epic. We hardly thought of prison: we told ourselves that they could not put a whole nation behind barbed wire, that since all France had been taken into custody it hardly mattered where we were, that it was better to rest at Auray than to tire ourselves out on the roads. We did not yet know that France was going to become one big cage.

Cepi's first concern, as might be guessed, was to take us to the local army headquarters. As we approached the military buildings our sergeant recovered his lightheartedness. Fresh energy pulsed through his limbs and heart; our barrack-room Antaeus was coming back to life. The prospect of some authority (even if a captive one) and discipline (even if without any object) brought him back to earth. For a week he had been wandering about through interstellar space from which customary values had disappeared and in which he felt ill at ease, despite his male assurance and his pleasure at being responsible for us. Only very strong souls can adapt themselves to the destruction of law and order, to the reign of anarchy. Cepi's soul, as far as I can judge fifteen years later, was that of an average man of the twentieth century, a Frenchman quite typical of his time, formed by the customs and traditions of his country, and above all accustomed to obedience and to ready-made ways of behavior suited to every circumstance. The faintheartedness which results from such experience is accentuated by the laws of military life: even narrower than the laws of civilian life, they leave the individual soldier with practically no initiative—tend to transform him into a mere cog in an indestructible machine. Ten months of regimental life had sufficed to make Cepi a real soldier—that is, a man lost if alone, in love with discipline despite his independent airs. This was how Cepi felt and acted while in uniform. (Afterward, I suppose, he had no difficulty in reassuming the soul of a civilian and quite naturally resumed making his own decisions and leading his own life with a certain degree of independence.)

Cepi's cheerfulness communicated itself to us; we looked with great pleasure at the barracks of Auray filled with French soldiers but guarded by German sentinels. I seem to remember the building as a big, flat structure of rough, gray stones. Inside, there was a great deal of animation. A number of men were swarming about. The soldiers looked as if they were on a holiday. They walked about the courtyard with their hands in their pockets. There were bunches of them at the windows smoking cigarettes and laughing. Cepi could hardly contain himself for joy. We were welcomed with much interest. Seeing us arrive at the gates of the barracks, some of the soldiers gave us mock salutes and mildly teased us.

A few—but they were very rare—expressed surprise that men who had had the chance of remaining free should come voluntarily to give themselves up. This attitude shocked Cepi and astonished the rest of us. As we saw it, it was they who were lucky: to be part of a proper unit, to have a roof over their heads, to get two regular meals a day, and to share a communal life. They did not know what misery it was to be a tramp without commander or objective.

"We will go and report," said Cepi. "After that we've nothing more to worry about."

# II

## *THE BELT*

In these enemy-controlled barracks the military machine was still functioning under French direction. We went through various formalities in order to be taken in, but I have forgotten what they were. At last we got to the supplies depot. There I had a peculiar desire which reminds me that I was only twenty—that is, at an age to be attached to material things. I wanted a lovely new belt in light-colored leather like ones I had admired on the tunics of certain privileged soldiers. The belt handed out to me when I had first joined up dated back to the 1914 war. It was blackened by use and

I was ashamed of it. Nothing could be more absurd than such a desire, but I do not regret it since it produced a charming memory.

There were several soldiers ahead of me. The corporal in charge was distributing his supplies under the control of an officer. This corporal was a small, jolly man who accompanied his gifts with amusing or agreeably grumpy remarks. When it came to my turn, I said, "I need a belt. I've lost mine."

I immediately regretted those rash words, for they unleashed signs of insane fury in the corporal, while the officer bridled and fixed me with a cold stare. I was now worried, and with my hands behind my back shifted uneasily from one foot to the other.

"Good God Almighty," yelled the corporal. "A belt! A smart aleck, eh? The gentleman says he has lost his belt. Who the devil wished this damn fool on me? Do you know where it lands you, losing military equipment, fathead? You don't know, you poor fish? Well, I'll tell you: it lands you in the guardhouse. Since you've lost your belt, you can now do without one, my good friend. Don't expect me to give you another. What the devil next! A man who loses his belt and then comes along and announces it as cool as you like. . . ."

Thereupon the officer treated me to a homily which made it clear that I was quite lucky (the very words he used) things were so unfortunate for the country as otherwise the business of the belt would have gone far, and that I would be well advised to get out of his sight with no further ado.

While the officer was talking I heard the supply corporal grumbling behind my back. Suddenly I felt a round rough object pushed into my hands and heard him saying in a tone of extraordinary affection, "Stuff that into your pocket, sonny, and get out of here quick."

The object was a new belt, rolled around its brass buckle. I still have it.

Before withdrawing I managed to whisper an energetic thank you to the corporal. The picture I carried away from this episode was of his wonderful smile. It was a confidential smile, a smile of connivance, a marvelous smile that made me happy for a week, a smile I have never forgotten, which has remained in my heart as a friendly symbol of human brotherhood and of the bantering kindness of the French people. There are some smiles which accompany one throughout a whole life. The good smile of the corporal of Auray, who so effectively hoaxed his officer and so adroitly kept faith with the fellowship of the lowly, will remain with me, I am sure, until my dying day. It is little things like that which make one love one's fellow men instead of loathing them.

# III

## *OLD MOTHER COCO*

I have said that the military machine continued to function. Actually, it functioned in a most extravagant manner. Although we were prisoners and guarded by Germans, the French commander of the barracks granted us midnight passes, which meant the German sentinel would open the gates for us if he were shown a piece of paper he could not understand. Cepi, who had not yet quite detached himself from us, got us passes for the night of our arrival.

He was anxious to show us that he had left a great impression in Auray and knew everything the town was capable of providing; for that reason he spent the first evening with us. During our wanderings he had told us a lot about a tavern kept by a sort of old provincial music-hall artist where he used to meet girls who had thrown their caps over the windmill. We had heard so much about this modest establishment that it had come to assume legendary proportions in our minds. Its owner, whom Cepi called "Old Mother Coco," seemed to us an entrancing person, half procuress and half provincial muse, a blasé lady of wit who had now retired to the country. Of course, we found nothing like this, nor was there any evidence of the abandoned hussies whom we had counted on for fabulous draughts of pleasure.

Mother Coco turned out to be a rather thin woman of about fifty, with platinum hair, and wearing a dress with a flowery pattern. She unquestionably had an air of distinction and was even intelligent. The way in which she said cordially but without any exaggerated emotion, "Hullo, Cepi. It's nice to see you again. What have you been doing the last three months?" seemed to me the quintessence of good manners. Her subsequent conversation and the protective and kindly way in which she questioned us youngsters denoted a woman of the world, a lady who had suffered reverses and had by no means always been an innkeeper. She had that slightly skeptial turn of mind, that faculty for subtle allusion, and that disillusioned tolerance which many French people had before the war, people who were fed on the *Oeuvre* and educated about life and men by a weekly reading of the *Canard Enchaîné*. This kind of democrat no longer exists. It is true that such reading did not produce very energetic temperaments, but it did prevent the semi-intellectuals from being as stupid as they are today.

# IV

## *REALISM*

It was from Mother Coco that I heard for the first time of General de Gaulle. She had listened to the broadcast appeal of June 18, 1940. This major event in our recent history had not, I must admit, made a big impression upon me. The name of De Gaulle seemed odd to me: I did not in the least grasp the full significance of his proclamation and his decision to carry on the war in the name of our country. My comrades and Cepi shared my indifference: we were much more interested in Pétain, who had put an end to an untenable situation by signing the armistice. Thanks to him, everything would be all right and soon we should be back in our dearly beloved civilian life. In short, to use a word that had much currency afterward, we were realists. We preferred to adapt ourselves to reality rather than to change it.

Most of the time the word *realism* is a polite translation of the word *cowardice*. There is no doubt that for the "realists" actions like those which cost the Chevalier d'Assas his life are models of absurdity. In the most favorable circumstances, realism leads to mediocrity; in the least favorable (and they are the most frequent) realism leads to the tomb.

There are circumstances in which prudence is the worst of follies. Almost nothing that great men have achieved is realistic. It is through realism, through lack of imagination, that men accept slavery. By virtue of the maxim that "it is better to be a live dog than a dead lion," which is the philosophic basis of political realism, men do descend to the level of dogs, which is precisely our level today; and men console themselves with the thought that even if they have to wear a collar and be kicked in the ribs, at least they are fed and sometimes patted. But this is a great fraud, because all the lions do not die. Forever live Achilles, who preferred thirty years of glory to a hundred years of an obscure existence!

France was still Achilles in 1914 but has since chosen the part of Nestor; and the Nestor she is acting is not even worthy of respect, being a senseless old fool confusing prudence with senility. Despite our youth, my four buddies, Cepi, and I had Nestorian souls, very old and very chickenhearted. Like Pétain, we wanted "to save what could be saved." A fine program that was! What was there to save? Nothing any more. Or rather, yes, there was still one thing, something we had not thought of: our souls. Unhappily, most men never think of their souls. General de Gaulle thought of his, but as for myself, the thought only struck me a year later. A case of belated thinking if there ever was one!

# V

## *WISE*
## *AFTER*
## *THE EVENT*

Not only was I, in my twentieth year, in the month of June, 1940, a victim of the detestable habit of being wise after the event, but I believe the whole of France was in its hold. The country was crushed, afflicted with total idiocy, understanding nothing about what was happening to it, interpreting everything the wrong way, believing that the moon is made of green cheese, disputing the most obvious truths, denying the most patent evidence.

As for myself, "young little mouse that had not seen a thing yet," I looked at everything with great curiosity but quite uncritically. I looked at it as an artist—that is to say, taking pleasure in the picturesque—but not as a historian or philosopher.

Events developed before our eyes as if they did not concern us, as if we were mere spectators. Defeat, collapse, invasion, and captivity were merely a game in which we took part with good grace and which had no importance. After all, as we said at the time, "the

*Boches* behaved correctly," and the good manners
with which they abstained from stamping on our
toes and hitting us with their rifle butts reassured
us completely. We found that we did not have to
deal with a horde of savages after all, that civilization had not been destroyed, that France went on.
In a month's time we would be back at our beloved jobs, we would again be carpenters, electri-
cians, butchers, and lawyers. We would be war
veterans like our fathers (but we promised to be
more modest about it). The *Boches* had robbed
us? Just a minute, the last word had not yet been
spoken. There was a second trick, a diplomatic
trick, to be won, and we held marked cards. Our
king of hearts was called Pétain. That wily old fox
would put Hitler in his pocket: because he was
handsome, because he was touching, because he
was old. Pétain, the Père Goriot of France, the
Christ of patriotism, had made us a gift of himself. France was the daughter of this blameless old
patriarch—a prodigal, a shameful daughter. She
threw herself into his arms and begged forgiveness
with great sobs for having read too many novels.
They were the explanation of why a big brute
had beaten her black and blue, poor thing.*

* After the collapse of 1940,
the Vichy regime organized a press campaign to tell France
that the real authors of the defeat were Marcel Proust and
André Gide. It appeared that their works had been read
too much and insidiously had infused into the national
soul the poison of renunciation and skepticism, so that our
armies had been crushed.
This foolishness was repeated
every day for four years. The purpose of such accusations is

It seems to me that if a serious historian one day undertakes the task of recording the war of 1940 and the years of the Occupation, he will constantly have to underline this belated thinking, this being wise after the event, which was rampant everywhere in France and which, I am afraid, was in the last analysis only one more proof of the state of stupidity into which the French had fallen. The line of duty was clearly drawn, and the attitude to be adopted was obvious; but people looked elsewhere. The prisoners did not understand that they were going to be locked up, the French did not grasp that having been defeated they were going to be treated accordingly and that the youthful Hitler was going to fool the aged Pétain. The relief of being beaten, the happiness of being reduced to inactivity, the voluptuous satisfaction of no longer being master of one's destiny and carrying this worrying responsibility, drowned the French conscience in delicious renuciation. We were ripe for slavery. We sighed for chains. We had done our best to obtain them.

Nothing is so ridiculous as a man afflicted with the malady of belated

clear: it is to make intelligence responsible for stupidity, to place on its shoulders crimes of which it is innocent in order to whitewash the fools who really committed the crimes. On this subject, as on so many others, Rivarol has said the last word. To some idiot of the emigration who said to him, "You will at least agree, sir, that intelligence has done us a lot of harm," Rivarol replied, "Why did you allow it to do so?"

thinking, the man who always has good ideas *too late*. I confess I was that man: patriotism, by which I mean active, intolerant, cruel, and effective patriotism, only came to me two years after the defeat; and of course the acts to which it led me were more difficult and more dangerous than the simple tasks of war would have been, had I made war befittingly. What I am saying here about myself is what, I believe, the whole of France can say about itself, with this difference: that I had a head which forced me to opt for difficulty and peril despite my natural laziness and cowardice, so that I managed to accomplish my own personal salvation. However, for a long time now my country has not had the kind of head which dictates bold actions and with which it could reconquer its conscience. It has been lurking on the back stairs for years, half asleep, its mind a blank, incapable of reflection, merely able to repeat, as it goes down the steps that lead to hell, "But I did not intend this . . ."

# VI

## *FIRST TWINGES OF THE SPIRIT OF CONTRADIC-TION*

What usually saves one from being wise after the event is possession of a spirit of contradiction. But that spirit is not at everybody's command. To contradict supposes an assertion of personality, even if an obstinate and stupid personality. It is a form of daring and non-conformity. Some quick-tempered souls with a bit of imagination who had followed the vicissitudes of the war without concern and without worrying much about the outcome, who had forgotten that the very life of the nation is at stake when one is fighting for the nation, suddenly, madly, began to regret the loss of their country. Their spirit of contradiction had prevented them from taking the official war seriously; it now began to prevent them from acquiescing in the official defeat to which the country as a whole was settling down so easily and so quickly. As far as I was concerned, I felt the first twinges of the spirit of contradiction in the middle of July 1940. Having been a prisoner of war for three weeks, and having disdained ten magnificent opportunities to escape, I suddenly saw the light; I made a wonderful discovery and said to myself, "The only duty of a prisoner of war is to escape." From then on I never ceased repeating these words until at last I did escape.

At that period, German soldiers inspired me with no particular horror, merely with a little curiosity; but I was responsive to the change in our situation. As long as the government was making war I was a pacifist. When it made peace and preached friendship with our enemies of yesterday, patriotism started to stir in my soul. For a whole year it only ventured out on occasional, timid and, I would even say, negative movements, producing in me a few protests and criticisms, leading me to take part in ostentatious collections for the Jews, etc., until the day came when I at last fully realized the real horror and absurdity of our condition.

# VII

## *THE GAMBLE*

Obviously the only man of France who was not afflicted with belated thinking was General de Gaulle. Whatever consideration dictated his appeal of the month of June—audacity, honor, desperation, or merely clear-sightedness—even the blindest will see, with the passage of time, that this appeal was the only possible thing to do because it was the most difficult thing to do. When in doubt, one must always choose the greatest difficulty. It is more difficult to fight than to capitulate, to repudiate a defeat than to accept it. The appeal of June 18, the only permissible attitude after the prostration of the French army, shows that General de Gaulle was the last Frenchman left with any true instinct, and that his instinct was sound and generous.

On the one side there was refinement, elegance, conformity, and realism. This was Vichy, toward which rushed everything France contained in the way of eminent minds, accomplished politicians, and ambitious soldiers. On the other side there was the absurd, the apparently useless gesture, the conventional attitude of the elementary-school textbooks on civic behavior. This was De Gaulle, upright on the small island of Britain and calling France to arms. How instructive the contrast is. All the prudence of Vichy and its sagacious calculations have gone down the drains of history. On the other hand, the useless and insane gesture, the simple-minded image and the textbook morality, have triumphed over misfortune.

Like the great artists, De Gaulle was not afraid of ridicule. Solitary and misunderstood, he did not fear being several years ahead of his time. In fact, again like the great artists, he was not ahead of his time; he simply saw clearly; it was the time that lagged behind. His time was being wise after the event. Men of genius, whatever they are—soldiers, statesmen, or poets—arrive at a moment when they feel sure of what is in their hearts, and then they let the heart speak first, before the intelligence. For De Gaulle this moment came on June 18, 1940, after the death of his country, as it came for Rembrandt after the death of his wife. Such a change does not take place without causing a great upheaval: it marks the passage from talent to genius; it announces the work and its future triumph. I feel so strong a tenderness for De Gaulle on the threshold of his change that I do not know how to describe it. I imagine him a prey to terrible apprehension, to that crisis of conscience which suddenly confronts a creator with the essential, and the need to give it shape. I imagine him a prey to the terror of the monk about to pronounce his vows and renounce the joys of this world. One is apt to forget that this great figure, this splendid monolith, also had his personal problems. On June 17 De Gaulle was a brilliant general and a judicious undersecretary of state. He was entitled, after many years of obscurity, to look forward to a distinguished military and political career. In the place of tangible goods and honors, the normal crown of a middle-class career (which neither Admiral Darlan nor General de Laurencie nor General Bridoux, nor a hundred others could resist), he preferred a task most hazardous, he preferred one small word; *honor*. This great soul, this noble and unique soul whom people have laughed at so much (as they laughed at the music of Beethoven and the painting of Renoir), despised honors and riches; he despised mere cleverness and even power. For quite minor exploits Louis XV gave the château of Chambord to Marshal de Saxe. General de Gaulle, whom they accuse of aspiring to dictatorship, lives today in Lorraine in a small house not even given to him by the State. This soldier from the conservative side in politics gives us a truly antique example of republican virtue. But where in the world are there any republicans left? Possibly in the kingdom of England there may be a few.

On June 17, 1940, De Gaulle had to choose between two roads: he could return to France and at last exercise his talents as a general and cabinet minister, or he could throw himself into a foolish enterprise. Very few soldiers or civilians responded to his appeal of June 18. Imagine that there had been fewer still. Imagine that there had been none. Imagine that, as Europe and America expected, the Germans had landed in Great Britain. In that case De Gaulle would have remained in an obscure corner of history with his impotent appeal and his empty words. As for the man himself, if he had not been killed, he would have been called for the rest of his life a scatterbrain, an idealistic fool, a malcontent, a sort of Ferdinand Lop in uniform. If Britain had been invaded, De Gaulle the braggart would have been reduced to blowing his brains out or taking flight to New York, where he would have dragged out a miserable existence on half pay in a shabby uniform and down-at-the-heel shoes. I am sure that he conjured up this picture of himself as an out-of-work staff officer in the midst of the vast indifference of the New World. I am sure he looked with a calm eye upon a destiny calculated to strike terror into smaller minds: I am sure he accepted possible martyrdom as the end most dignified for a man who insisted on standing upright when his country had lain down. When a great man finds himself placed in mediocre circumstances—in other words, when he is the last man to be standing upright in a country brought low by shame and stupidity—all he desires is an ignominious death. His superior morality demands this. It is the stake of Joan of Arc. It is the firing squad of Rossel at the camp of Satory. I have said that there comes a moment in the lives of men of genius when the heart takes over command from the brain. At this moment they engage in a gamble with fate, of which the stake is their whole life's work, of which the stake is their very selves. If they win, it is glory. If they lose, it is death or misery. And there never is a way of avoiding the gamble: the devil is there in attendance to burn the bridges and the boats, to compel the man of genius to throw everything onto the green baize cloth, to give up everything;

the devil is there to insist upon the supreme act of courage.

This courage, which one of our compatriots had in the month of June 1940, is the only thing that today can still provide us with some pride in being French. It is the only ray of sunshine that has warmed us for fifteen years. At least there lives one great soul in France. The French people, this people which *was great,* as Stendhal and Gobineau said even in their time, and which has become so small, was still able to draw from its tired womb one of the finest characters of our age.

# VIII

## *A COUNT MAKES A COUNTESS*

I owe Mother Coco this tribute: she did not make any mistake about General de Gaulle. She talked to us about him with interest and a kind of respect. She had been moved by the speech of June 18. It had been pronounced in a strange, pompous voice that let phrases drop as if they were balls of lead. It had been badly transmitted by a wireless plagued with atmospheric difficulties. But she *attached importance to it*. With her instinct, she sensed that it was not a case of just a lot of words—but that there was already a situation *behind* the words. France was no longer entirely defeated, for one of her sons had announced his determination to go on fighting to the end. General de Gaulle spoke with a mixture of passion and contempt which roused a desire both to follow him and to hate him. The virture expressed by his voice was no amiable virtue. One imagined a leader stiff, inflexible, and not in the least good-natured. In his favor were only his courage and the romance of being beyond the seas and contradicting the government and defying destiny.

On the other side of the coin was the ancient siren Pétain, bleating out spacious and appeasing words. He chided us affectionately. He was sad and gentle. It is difficult for a man of eighty not to inspire some affection. Alas, it was to this good and indulgent grandpa that the hearts of the French went out. Pétain's glory was a thing of the past. It no longer frightened anybody. It was a restful glory. Verdun seemed as far off as Wagram or Tolbiac. With Pétain, the history of France rose from its tomb to take us by the hand and console us for our present misfortunes. For those who mistake their memories for rights, how restful and convenient a forgotten war, a buried victory, can be. It provides all the advantages of glory without any of the fatigue of acquiring it.

But history is a shadow; the past is deceptive. One must deserve one's past (as much as one's future) if it is to be of any use; failing this, the past is one more millstone, an extra shackle snapped around the ankle of the slave. In choosing Pétain, the French chose their dead glory, their assured and facile glory. De Gaulle represented an uncertain glory, something that had still to be born. History, of course, was on the side of De Gaulle. After it has been made, history seems infinitely seductive; when it is in the making it has a repellent look. People laughed at General de Gaulle's voice. They complained about his hostile tone, his stiffness, his coldness. But De Gaulle was issuing a call to arms. He was making history. This was not the moment to relax. That icy voice, that emphatic tone, those heavy words he threw at us like a box on the ears—they were the voice, the tone, the very words of history. Without this damnable business of belated thinking we would have realized all that. It is no good denying it: on June 18, 1940, France was afraid of history; or she did not know how to recognize it, which comes to the same thing. France behaved like a middle-class father who prefers to marry off his daughter to the incapable heir of an established fortune rather than to a young man of talent who doesn't have a penny, according to the maxim that a clever husband does not make his wife clever, but a count makes his wife a countess. The penalty for this kind of behavior comes soon enough: the incapable rich man ruins himself within four years while the young man of talent emerges from the shadows.

One sometimes loses if one bets, but one is always the loser if one never dares gamble at all. That is the moral we ought to keep in mind whenever there is a serious decision to be taken. It is the moral of audacity.

# IX

## COPS AND ROBBERS

I was thinking none of these thoughts, of course, when I was twenty, sipping the champagne offered us by Mother Coco in the inn at Auray to celebrate her reunion with Cepi. No, I was rather happy; I felt myself surrounded by friendliness; for a week I had had a lot of fun; I felt that at last everything would come out all right, as Pétain in his wisdom had put an end to the absurdities of war.

Childhood games tend to copy real life, but they do not have its tragic character since they are only games and can be stopped in time. Thanks to Pétain, the war, which so far had been a business of grownups who kill each other in earnest, became a huge game which was brought to a stop because night had fallen and the children had to go to bed. To me, to my comrades, and to the majority of the soldiers shut up in Auray, this change seemed marvelous. We welcomed it with enthusiasm. No more need, henceforth, to look after ourselves. Pétain was a second father who was taking matters in hand and, like all grownups, would give them a reasonable solution—that is, a solution of weakness. After having played for a few days at being a man, I found myself thrown back into my childhood. I shall never be tired of repeating that young people are timid; only half out of their childhood, they still retain many of childhood's prejudices and terrors. The impetuousness and the spirit of adventure often attributed to young people exist only in the parrotlike imagination of bad novelists.

To what extent the war and the defeat had—thanks to the broadcast homilies of Marshal Pétain—become a sort of game, was proved by the escapade with which our visit to Mother Coco ended. We had been in the inn for about three quarters of an hour, listening admiringly to Mother Coco and Cepi passionately exchangingly insignificant bits of news, when we heard a German patrol coming up the street in marching step. I do not know what demon seized hold of us: all six of us jumped up, and without a word Mother Coco took us into the back parlor. The patrol entered the inn. Fifteen years after this event, I still do not understand it: we had proper passes and the right, endorsed by the German sentinel at the barracks, to be out till midnight. That Mother Coco hid us is understandable: she knew nothing about our having passes and perhaps thought, in her straightforward, womanly way, that we wanted to escape; but why did we allow ourselves to be hidden? Whichever way you look at it, it was absurd. I suppose that unconsciously we felt obliged to play at cops and robbers. Showing us into the back parlor, Mother Coco whispered, "There is a door at the end of the corridor. It is the back entrance and opens into the other street." All this fake romanticism about nothing at all ought to have brought us to our senses.

We no doubt made a little noise with our hobnail boots, because when we reached the door the patrol in the barroom started shouting in German, and we heard heavy feet starting to run. We hurried out into the street, turned two or three corners, and took refuge in a house which had its door open. Two minutes later the patrol passed by on the double in a hubbub of nailed boots, clanking of firearms, and German cries. The noise died down. Our hearts were beating fast. Was it emotion or shortness of breath? We looked at each other. "Phew," said Cepi, pretending to wipe his brow and shake a hand dripping with sweat. We broke into laughter. Here we were, involved in an escape without even wanting it. One step more and we would have been free men. But the idea of taking this step never occurred to us. What it is to lack imagination!

We stayed at Auray several days. We often went for walks in the town; we could have escaped again and again; all we had to do was not go back to the barracks at night. Who today can understand such crazy behavior? Yet it was how we did behave. It seemed like the most natural thing in the world and, what is more, the wisest.

"Children," said Cepi, "I suggest we get back to the barracks now. We've done enough for today."

The streets were swarming with German patrols and even with French ones; our silly game made it a duty to avoid them. At the barracks there was no difficulty about getting in; our passes were in order. When we entered our dormitory, a soldier called out, "Well, we never thought we'd see you again. Why didn't you beat it, with your passes?"

"Why should they beat it?" asked another soldier. "In a fortnight they'll be demobbed and their journey home will be paid for."

This was the first time I heard talk about a paid journey home. It was not the last. I was to hear this remark dozens of times a day all the time I was a prisoner. Weeks passed by, England was never invaded, peace never came, and discipline became more and more tyrannical, but nothing lessened the appeal of the free trip home.

It was because of this, and in the teeth of all the evidence, that five hundred thousand men refused to escape. What did the famous journey home cost in 1940? Possibly a hundred francs for some, fifty francs for others. This was the price, laughable even for poor men, which a third of the French army placed on its freedom—and it found even that expensive.

# X

## *FRIENDSHIP AND THE OPEN SKY*

I do not remember much about the town of Auray. Of this landscape which, as I say, ought to have been graven on my memory, there remains only the blue and white sky, the sky of all Brittany in the summer. The solid, gray, granite houses have dissolved, and I recall with difficulty the streets full of French and German soldiers, the light dresses of the Breton women, and the shops. But without any effort I can see above my head the azure blue of the month of June 1940 and the white, flaky, clearly defined clouds, their curves accentuated by shadows; I can still feel the very hot sun on my cheeks; I can still smell the scent of wet dog that my tunic gave off when it rained.

There are countries (and times) when the temperature is very important. Although I am a poor hand at remembering facts and names I do at any rate remember the state of my feelings. At twenty I was continually verifying the famous statement of Amiel: "A landscape is a state of mind." Nature engraved itself on my heart as surely as a melody would have, or the perfume of a desirable woman. When all is said and done, there is no better picture of my state of mind in June 1940 than the sky and the heat of Auray. I was undoubtedly closer to the elements than I am today, or more sensitive to their influence. In the same way (was it due to the circumstances or to my youthful age?) I felt I was a friend of everyone; I welcomed each encounter with sincere pleasure and cordiality. I had no more critical sense than a poplar. I fed on everything, and naturally everything "agreed" with me.

Proofs of the sympathy of my fellows were not lacking. If I wished, I could draw up quite a long list of those gifts which consist of a look of confidence or a cordial smile. Such small effusions have always moved me so strongly that it takes little more to bring tears to my eyes. I admit that this sensibility is a little silly; but it may be inseparable from a kind of vocation I have for friendship and faithfulness. It is often argued, in this epoch of intellectual confusion, that friendship is nothing but love gone cold. This does not agree with my own experience; I see a difference in kind between the two feelings. Friendship is a pure passion into which enters no kind of physical desire, conscious or unconscious. There is nothing lukewarm about it, either. People have been known to get themselves killed for the sake of friendship, while there have been lovers who had absolutely no feeling of friendship for the object of their love.

My twentieth year was really illuminated with friendship. I found it everywhere and at every instant. Never so much as at that moment of my life did I feel my interdependence with my unhappy countrymen who had been thrown back upon each other by the waves of Germans pouring in over our country. I must make it clear, however, that I only had dealings with people of modest condition, subject to the blows of fate because of their lowly estate and their lack of means. I suppose that people who were well off, who had "something to save," who thought of preserving their goods and their comfort, would not have offered me anything of the kind.

# XI

## A VERY
## SIMPLE STORY

Here is an incident which, by some miracle, I have not forgotten and which, I believe, illustrates all this rather well. It is a touching anecdote, a bit simple perhaps, in the style of Alphonse Daudet or Legouvé. Its hero is an old man I met during one of those extravagant midnight leaves which the French officer in charge of the camp went on giving us—in the hope, perhaps, that we would take advantage of them to escape—and which the German commander countersigned with a confidence he was not mistaken in placing in us.

For once I had gone out without my buddies, prey to a longing for solitude which takes hold of me from time to time and which used to even at the age of fifteen. Solitude produces a special exaltation which seems to me a state of happiness, a vacancy of the mind and heart propitious to the most captivating adventures. I was walking along without any special place to go, picking up noises as a flower picks up pollen, watching, so to speak, my scattered ideas and feelings fall into place inside myself, and feeling a deep joy at observing the involuntary order establishing itself in my head and heart. It was in this state of bliss that the old man found me. He was coming along toward me slowly, heedlessly, enjoying his solitude as I was enjoying mine, but he had evidently been at it longer than I, since he was now anxious for company. You could feel an air of curiosity in him, an air of asking questions. In short, he was a man who wanted to chat a little with a stranger. When he reached me, he called out, "Are you hungry, soldier?"

I was not hungry, but I read in his eyes that he wanted to give me something to eat. He was one of those peasants of whom it is difficult to say whether they are beggars or farmers. I believe this one was really poor. He was wearing a worn-out velvet coat from which the buttons had fallen off like dried nuts, a pair of patched pantaloons, down-at-the-heel shoes, and a greasy old cap. His face has vanished from my mind. I only remember his smile, which was very luminous and a bit simple.

"I could do with a bite," I told him.

"Come along then," he said, producing part of a two-pound loaf of bread and a piece of gelatinous pig's-head *pâté* like a jellyfish wrapped up in paper. "What do you say to that? You'll like it. Where are you from?"

"From Paris," I replied.

"Well, you won't get grub like this in Paris, believe me. What do you say to the two of us eating it someplace where we can wash it down with some wine?"

"Now there's a fine idea," I exclaimed with well-simulated delight.

"All right, let's go then," the old man said.

This picture is followed by another one. We are sitting at a table under an arbor. The sun has sunk quite low but it is still very warm; it is five or six in the afternoon. Wild vine or convolvulus must have been intertwined with the arbor, for I remember very clearly wavering spots of sunshine on the table and on my companion's coat. (I was completely crazy, at that period, about impressionist painting: I thought of the forest interiors of Claude Monet and of Renoir's *Moulin de la Galette*. These pedantic reminiscensces of the young artist who can never resist comparing nature with the manner in which great men have rendered it gave me much pleasure and a very good opinion of my sensitivity.) The old man and I are thoughtfully munching the pig's-head *pâté* and the homemade bread. Between us on the table are two glasses and a bottle of harsh red wine. The *pâté* is fatty and nauseating and it seems to me we'll never come to the end of it. I try to take as little as possible but each time I finish one portion the old man insists on my helping myself again. We cut this food with our dark-bladed pocketknives pressed against our thumbs.

"Go on eating," says the old man. "At your age you have to eat. Do you get enough to eat in Paris? Pretty good, eh, my *pâté?* Go on, wade in. What you eat today nobody can take away from you. Go on, have a drink, it's on me. And you must finish the bread. You don't think I'm going to take any of it back home, do you?"

# XII

## *BEGINNING OF A CHANGE*

Memory cuts across recollections the way good novelists cut short the scenes of their stories—that is, as soon as the essential has been said. At this point the hospitable old man disappears from my mind. How did I leave him? How did I thank him? Knowing myself, I must have overflowed with gratitude and friendliness, must have expressed myself effusively, and embraced him. In saying good-by to him I probably thought sadly that I would never again meet this heart of gold, and that life was very hard. I always used to be seized with violent regrets whenever the thought came to me that I might never again meet a particular person who had been good to me or toward whom my heart had gone out. I can see now that this was a form of that detestable spirit of possessiveness which we can sometimes free ourselves from and replace, if we have sufficient wisdom, with a spirit of detached enjoyment.

We should gratefully accept what men offer and not want any more from them or from destiny. We should always remember how fragile human affections are; we should feel to the very roots of our souls how temporary our condition is; we should know that nothing can be preserved forever. These are ideas which make life infinitely easier but which are acquired only with effort. To enjoy without the desire to possess seems to me, at the age I have now reached, a good compromise between paganism and the Christian ethic. It permits enjoyment of the best of people and things unshadowed by fear of losing them. It is the first step on that pleasant road which leads to the death of the passions.

The story of the old man and the *pâté* is revealing, for if in 1940 I was quick to become emotional, I was also quick to scoff. I hated people who had "the soil of France clinging to the soles of their boots," and nothing exasperated me more than "the old peasant." I was ignorant of almost everything, I was lacking in imagination, I had not yet learned courage, but I was not stupid and I thoroughly hated the nonsense fed to me in my childhood. The conventional picture of the old peasant, who dragged himself through the mediocre poems of the nineteenth century, was perhaps the one which provoked the greatest dislike in me. Yet when he turned up in the flesh, dressed in tattered velvet as in the Comtesse de Ségur, I did not recognize him. I welcomed him as something marvelously new, as an opportunity for an intoxicating experience of friendship. The times must indeed have been exceptional. What a complete change was going on inside me!

# XIII

## *LAZINESS*

The change in myself was proceeding in step with the change taking place in my country. But while I had plenty of interest in watching the latter, the insidious progress inside myself escaped me. My mind was occupied with the discoveries I was making every minute about the world and the people in it. I did not know that my heart was secretly at work.

At Auray, I had an ineffaceable and ferociously precise foretaste of captivity. Returning to the barracks in the evening, I no longer found the calm, well-ordered world of the army but a sort of hypocritical village fair. The rooms already had that impoverished bohemian look of prisoners' huts. As Auray contained far more German and French soldiers than it could hold, triple tiers of beds had been built to crowd in as many men as possible. The prisoners lazed their days away in a state of idleness greater even than that accompanying active war service. They had only to attend roll call and do a few fatigues. This made for a delightful life consisting of card parties alternating with prolonged siestas on straw mattresses.

From the first day of the defeat the men wore their uniforms in the most unorthodox ways, outdoing each other in their efforts to look like tramps. But even more than the appearance of the men and the barracks, it was the sheer laziness by which my comrades suddenly found themselves petrified that gave me my first idea of what our existence was henceforth going to be: an endless and unbearable idleness. That is, at any rate, what the officers experienced for five years. The lower ranks were subjected to various peaceful tasks, highly degrading for men who had been taken from their trades and sent to fight. If the soldiers mobilized in September 1939 had been told that for five years they were going to be transformed into road-makers or agricultural laborers, what would they have said?

But in June 1940 nobody talked about anything except going home. Their legs crossed, their hands folded behind their heads, their caps pushed down over their eyes, wrapped up in dirty sweaters, my comrades lolled about, smiling, smoking black cigarette ends. Some had a worried look, but most of them were still in the good humor of men who have rid themselves of a great burden. As nobody felt responsible, the defeat could be enjoyed without mental reservations. (This statement, by the way, applies to the whole of France, including cabinet ministers and generals.) As one might guess, the prisoners of Auray did not stint themselves when it came to swearing and indignation. They drew graphic pictures of muddle in their regiments, of confusion in the moves they had been ordered to carry out, of the stupidities of the N.C.O.s, and so on. They overlooked only one thing: their own slackness. But, on reflection, I believe I am misjudging them. They had the modesty of the simple private who will obey any order and will not try to understand. If I remember rightly, they complained chiefly about the bad quality of their weapons. They did not say that with better arms and better chiefs they would have been good soldiers, but they sincerely thought so, and no doubt they were not mistaken. Men are neither lions nor sheep but a mixture of the two. It is the man who leads them who turns them into either lions or sheep.

# XIV

## *THE MIRACLE*

From the lowest rung of the army ladder on which I was standing in 1940 I could see the final consequences of the utter incompetence of the government and the general staff. General Gamelin and his subordinates seem to have been numskulls of the worst kind, incapable of any organization or of any plan, and incapable, of course, of the smallest act of boldness. Twenty-five years earlier, these timid functionaries—for whom the real theater of operations was the promotion roster—who had reached their eminence only by force of mediocrity, would have been superseded in twenty-four hours.

But France in 1939 did not have the reflex of patriotic defense she had had in 1914. There was nobody on top sufficiently powerful to ruthlessly throw out these useless Radical-Socialist or Fascist generals who had prospered like cockroaches between the disjointed floor boards of the Staff College. Instead, we had the deplorable spectacle of a war not conducted by, but inflicted upon, a group of poltroons anxious to be right after the event, men who had not even had misgivings about assuming the command. I do not know what the orders of the general staff had been, but I do at least know that at the lowest level of execution, where I stood, these orders had resulted in complete confusion. I suppose that what happened in 1939–1940 would also have happened in 1914, that we would have been swallowed up then in less than no time, if Joffre had not ruthlessly swept the feeble heads of the army into ignominious exile in the backwaters of Limoges, and if Galliéni had not counteracted the total incompetence of his colleagues with the taxis of Paris.

The miracle of the Marne prevents French generals from sleeping and even from thinking. But they must learn that miracles are the appendages of men of genius and not of imbeciles, and that it is ridiculous (and in this particular case fatal) to trust to one's genius when one has not got any.* In September 1939 the miracle would have been for a new Joffre to

* Why should fate bother to manufacture miracles for fools and cowards who in no way deserve them? Besides, miracles are only the invention of a lazy, defeatist spirit. A close look at the anatomy of the miracle and its forms of expression shows that nothing is less miraculous. Here are two small, true facts which, when multiplied by a hundred thousand, show what the miracle of the Marne was made of:

(1) At Saint-Denis, near Paris, the infantrymen crowded in taxis ready to leave saw a German *Taube* plane wheeling in the sky and fired their rifles at it.

(2) At the height of the battle of the Marne Julien Simon, colonel of a regiment of Senegalese, stationed himself between two ranks of gunfire, which obliged him after each burst to get off his horse at the risk of breaking his neck, for he kept losing his eyeglasses.

spring up from within the ranks of our regular army and relegate the unfortunate Gamelin and a hundred of his generals to some provincial backwater, with orders to write wise comments on the conduct of operations for provincial newspapers. Not even a Joffre was needed: just one obstinate general who understood that the role of an army is to march to the sound of guns—a truth that had been totally lost sight of. Given that understanding, miracles would have followed in quick succession. Our hundred and ten divisions would have carved up the twenty-three German divisions of the Siegfried line without great difficulty. We would have overrun Germany as quickly as the Germans overran France, and we would have been waiting in Berlin for Hitler to get back from Poland.

# XV

## *WISDOM*

The military tramps of Auray were certainly not pondering any such bold thoughts or feeling any such clearly defined regrets, but they knew that an enormous opportunity had been missed. Naturally they talked about treason and the Fifth Column. They chewed over their vague but vehement grievances. Whenever they spoke of the war they shrugged their shoulders or raised their eyes to heaven. They considered themselves victims, not guilty men. And they were not wrong. But the role of victim is a dangerous one; what is worse, they took pleasure in it. They were inaugurating five years of "victimitis." The cult of the martyr and of the glorious defeat has never been so much observed in France as since the war.

The German soldiers guarding us led a very active life. This small, compact force, armed to the teeth, never made a useless move. Compared to us, it was geometry opposed to chaos. I was curious about the Fritzes; in my simplicity of mind I thought they despised us. As a matter of fact, they noted our inactivity with pleasure. Their chiefs must have given them to understand that the more we were plunged in idleness, the more docile we would become. Apart from that, these Germans were wooden-headed idiots who could be divided into two categories: a minority of arrogant fellows who bullied us and a majority of good-natured men who did not give a fig for the war and the destiny of nations and who saw us only as unhappy fellow creatures. As for contempt, it was rather we who professed it for them. But this contempt did not exclude the ordinary admiration of the vanquished for his victor. We were impressed by their equipment, their discipline, the streamlined parades, the clicking of heels, the long-handled grenades stuffed into their boots, the short tunics with buttoned pockets, and the sporting air of the men. We watched it all with nostalgia, envy, mockery, anger, and grief. To think that we too could have been fine soldiers, disciplined and ferocious—because we would have been ferocious. We would have been true conquerors, violent, cruel, arrogantly trampling under foot the soil we conquered, taking the women and humiliating the men. We should never have been accused of behaving correctly!

We revenged ourselves for our admiration of our jailers by commenting on their ridiculous aspects (which, incidentally, boiled down to one thing: their goose step) and by holding our noses when they went by. It was a curious thing, this smell the Germans spread, which infested the barracks within a few hours. It was a sweetish, slightly sickly scent composed of boot grease and rifle oil, the smell of leather, sweat, soap, and Oriental tobacco. It had nothing in common with the scent of the French soldier, which is spiced and potent. Even beaten and a prisoner, the French soldier has about him the smell of a man and a warrior. The German soldier smelled like a barber's assistant or a rank boarding-school boy. This odor came from another planet. It was a severe, puritanical odor, an unbearable stench produced by virgin bodies fed on ersatz and potatoes. It seemed to put the seal on our downfall. This unknown odor, settling down on France and making us sick at our stomachs, showed better than anything else that we were no longer at home in our own country. Nevertheless, we considered ourselves superior to the German soldiers since we were only temporary prisoners and would soon be returning to civilian life. We were luckier than they.

Our defeat also inspired us with a truly strange pride: the mere fact of being there, locked up and reduced to impotence and meditation, made us regard ourselves as men of wisdom. When we looked at the Germans, so busy, so self-important, organizers of nothingness, and still subjected to the antics of military life, we took ourselves for adults looking with pity upon the follies of children. They still believed in war and in the army; we had outlived those stupidities a long time ago. We had refused to take part in that game. Being in some way the more intelligent, we had given way, as grownups give way to the whims of children, with a resigned smile and a shrug of the shoulders. We were so thoroughly steeped in these sentiments that they conferred a highly edifying dignity upon our attitude. The *Boches* must have considered us indomitable, since they read on our faces nothing but contempt and mild derision. I blush to think, fifteen years later, that there were perhaps some shrewd men among them. To those, our contempt and derision must have appeared highly comical.

# XVI

## *OPTIMISM*

It was at Auray, in June 1940, that for the first time optimism rose before me like a tempting devil. Up till then, trusting to Voltaire, I had loathed optimism. (I had only come across it in its family manifestations, where it was irritating but of little consequence.) At Auray, however, it took hold of me like an opium-eater's dream. Nearly all my comrades were optimistic. They believed firmly that the war was over and their liberation only a matter of days and a few formalities. They were getting ready to go back to their homes almost at once. Cheer up; everything is not black in a *lost* war. Suppose things had taken a different turn—months or years of fighting would have gone on, followed by more loss of time in occupying conquered territories. What a bore a victory is. Defeat removes all difficulties. In a fortnight we'll be embracing our wives and parents again.

These notions were based on such arguments as: Pétain "would not allow" Hitler to keep us in captivity; it was not "to Hitler's interest" to feed a million and a half idle mouths. Besides, the dearest desire of this same Hitler was to turn France into a friend. He was going to give all her children back to France as a gift. We should then understand that we had been mistaken all along about this gallant man. What a stroke of political genius it would be to release all his prisoners after two or three weeks! As for England, she would be invaded next week, and peace would be signed in July. We distinguished very clearly the difference between peace and an armistice. We wanted peace, a definitive peace; we wished for it intensely. Peace and demobilization. Being prisoners of recent date, we talked of *demobilization* and not of *liberation*. We were still using a prewar vocabulary.

Under these conditions, why escape? It would have been utter folly. However easy escape might be (and it was easy), it meant an "adventure," it means complications, spending money, maybe running into danger. And it might mean finding oneself in a rather delicate situation, one which would perhaps have to be regularized at some future time, and this, possibly, might not be easy to do. Who knows, it might mean being hunted, living the life of a man on the run, with the German and French police after one. The Germans, these "correct" people so full of confidence in us, might become difficult if their anger were aroused and they saw they had been flouted. They were decent fellows, of course, but they refused to joke about breaking army regulations. To escape might mean ending in a punishment camp, or even being shot.

The prophecies of the optimists always ended by conjuring up that *free trip home*. After all, it would be too unfair to have to spend fifty or a hundred francs returning home when one had not come here for one's own pleasure in the first place. These fifty or hundred francs broke the hearts of the prisoners. They wanted to go home at the cost of the government; they were all agreed upon that. They insisted on the journey back in a cattle truck that would not cost a sausage and that, furthermore, would be legal and without danger. They were absolutely sure of this free trip home: they had had, so to speak, a special revelation on the subject. It was no more than what was due them. In two or at most three weeks they would be clambering into trains, amid jokes and laughter, loaded down with the minor loot picked up during the retreat. The *Boche* sentinels would look at them with envious eyes. During the journey pints and pints of red wine would be drunk. The tragedy was going to have a happy ending: a return from holidays. Happiness is not so easily lost. It would be ours once more in the middle of July—strongly tainted with cowardice, no doubt, but you can't have something for nothing, and happiness is worth every sacrifice, including that of honor (which, incidentally, is the easiest sacrifice to make). And this didn't take into account the fact that the government and journalists would surely find a way of justifying us or even, if need be, supplying us with reasons for being proud of ourselves.

All this was pretty contagious. Influenced by Cepi and my four buddies,

I resolutely joined the ranks of the optimists. The few pessimists and their disillusioned remarks annoyed me. I kept away from them. They were too discouraging. It is true that they painted a picture of the future which turned out to be fairly accurate, predicting a long war, numerous privations, acute poverty, and seemingly endless captivity. But they made no effort to avoid this fate. That the optimists did nothing is not surprising: short-sighted sheep who from afar confuse hell and heaven and, bleating marching songs on the way, let themselves be led to the slaughterhouse. But how is the apathy of the pessimists to be explained? Were they not real pessimists? Were they pessimists only in appearance? Did they, at the bottom of their hearts, nurse the same hopes as the others? Ordinarily pessimism is a factor of energy, the source of all the virtues, the embryo of action. A man who foresees the worst can arm himself against it and conquer it; and as the worst does not always happen, the strength of this man often is greater than his victories demand. But what can be said for a pessimist who prepares for nothing? What can be said of a clear-sighted mind unsupported by generous ardor? This is the worst kind of coward: a sad coward, a consciously, irremediably defeated man. I must say I dislike the optimists less: their case is not hopeless. At Auray, pessimism engendered not the least spark of energy in its grumbling advocates. They had the sterile disillusionment of the family spoilsport— which is nothing but bad temper.

# XVII

## *ONE FOR ALL*
## *AND ALL*
## *FOR ONE*

Apart from my optimism, what kept me at Auray was friendship. I was very much attached to Cepi and my four buddies. They had become my brothers. We now shared eight days of tremendous memories. I imagine that Cepi, who knew life a little and had had other experiences, was less involved than we were, but as he had constituted himself our leader his attachment to us, although of another kind, was no less keen. We were convinced that the six of us formed a cell united forever by friendship and the tasks we had shared, and we could not imagine a future in which one of us would not be there. We were six persons with only one head and heart. For the first time I felt the intoxicating emotion of brotherhood of arms (even though the arms had been shattered). Not for anything in the world would I have left my friends. Freedom without them would have no savor or attraction; it would mean nothing. To abandon my friends to their fate, to be selfishly happy alone, would have seemed to me the height of sacrilege. Besides, I was by no means unhappy, and I would have been if free.

This blindness baffles me, even taking into account our youth (for I was not alone in feeling this way: my four buddies—and perhaps Cepi too—felt as I did). We obviously were in danger from one day to the next of being separated by our conquerors or the orderlies in charge of the dormitories, or of being dispersed to the four corners of Europe, thus rendering our fidelity useless. But our optimism was vigilant: peace was imminent. Till then we would surely find means of keeping together. Superstitiously, we relied as much on our friendship as on our brains. Afterward, when everything was over, when we were all back in Paris, we promised ourselves a lovely life, all six of us. First of all, we would buy ourselves a tremendous lunch at La Belle Aurore, a fashionable restaurant of the time.

I had this lunch at La Belle Aurore some months later, but with another buddy whom I did not yet know at this period. Eight or ten days sufficed to destroy our association, and another eight days for us to become perfect strangers. There indeed was a great experience, all within two weeks: friendship, and oblivion. It was not the least of the lessons I learned from my "months of campaigning."

# XVIII

## *EXIT CEPI*

The first to leave our small phalanx, as might have been guessed, was Cepi, who a few days after our capture bade us a very sentimental farewell. Finding the army again had given him back the good humor and activity we had seen him display in training camp before the disaster, when he was a brilliant sergeant who looked down on us from a great height, dropped us a word or two from time to time with a smile, and barely hid his contempt for the instructors who were corporals. For that matter, during the whole of our wanderings Cepi had never abandoned any of his smartness. He did not undo his tunic despite the heat and he always rolled his puttees in the N.C.O. manner—that is, by twisting them over at each turn of the leg. (This complicated and refined art calls for special puttees, much longer than the regulation ones and made of finer cloth.) As Cepi was fair, his beard, even when he had not shaved, barely showed. Compared to him, we were wretched looking. We had absolutely no idea of what being properly dressed soldiers meant and knew nothing of the modest neatness of men who have absorbed the tradition of the barracks. We were untidy and dirty, we affected the style of the old trooper, which must

147

have been rather comic. We had allowed ourselves to grow disgusting mustaches that looked like smears of dust across our childish faces.

At Auray Cepi rejoined his equals, noncommissioned officers who were below their proper rank, so to speak, and would have become captains if there had been any going to war at all. They were offhand and ironical. We felt they were full of experience of the army and life, and that made us jealous. Cepi held long secret meetings with them. Intrigued, we supposed that they were preparing great things together: slipping over to England perhaps. The idea of such daring frightened us, but it was annoying not to be in on the secret.

Then: "My lambs," Cepi told us, "the time has come to say good-by. I have asked to be transferred to the Senarmont quarter where I have friends. I have led you here: mission accomplished. You are safe. We certainly took a great walk together. It wasn't bad. On the contrary. But there's a time for everything. I'm no longer the right age to be a nursemaid. You give me your addresses, and we'll see each other again when it's all over. Now let us embrace each other."

We did embrace, and not without emotion. We were sad to see Cepi go. True, he had again become the sergeant, but his farewell speech was spoken with friendliness and that fraternal good humor which makes life between men so agreeable.

What still moves me about Cepi, even today, is that he had the jauntiness and irony of the French soldiers after Waterloo, as Stendhal has well described them in the first pages of *La Chartreuse de Parme*. Even after one hundred and twenty years, his language was the same as theirs. It was not so much the words he used as the way he put them together and the way his sentences followed one another. His speeches had a swaggering air, with ellipses and exclamations that would not have been in the least out of place in a description of war by Stendhal or Balzac. This dear fellow talked like a man who had behind him the campaigns of Italy and Egypt as well as the battles of Austerlitz and Moscow. His ancestral language pleased me very much. I saw in it a proof that France was not lost, and that, when everything was said and done, all we had lacked was a Napoleon. Since Cepi, who had nothing exceptional about him, used such appropriate and vigorous language, France must still have great resources of energy.

What became of Cepi I do not know. Did he go to England? Did the Germans enroll him by force in their army, since he was Alsatian? I seem to remember that he had a certain respect for our conquerors. This good soldier appreciated at its proper value the excellent order reigning in the *Wehrmacht*. In addition, he spoke German well and often talked with *Feldwebels* who had nothing to do. Whatever his fate,

I hope that our excellent comrade came out of it all right, that he is alive and happy in his work as a traveling salesman, and that he did not leave his blood and legs or arms outside Smolensk or at Bir Hakeim.

# XIX

## *DESPAIR*
## *AT THE*
## *ARSENAL*

Time and space march down the corridors of memory at the same pace. They shrink together. The places we lived in as children seem huge. We are surprised by their smallness twenty years later. In the same way, we think we were a long time in them when actually we spent only a few days there. This is because in childhood impressions are rich and numerous, and their traces are not wiped out. It is difficult to imagine that so many impressions could have been gathered in so short a time. My deceitful memory tells me that I stayed in Auray two or three weeks. In reality it was probably no more than three or four days. One morning we were ordered to get up at dawn and make up our packs. After standing for five hours hopping from one foot to the other, grumbling, we clambered onto trucks which took us at top speed, in the midst of clouds of dust, to Vannes under a very hot sun. The optimists thought this move was the first step toward freedom; the pessimists that it was another step toward servitude. As for me, I remember having felt happy because of the nut-tree branches which tickled our faces agreeably as we turned corners. The trucks rolled slowly through Vannes, so that the population was able to express sympathy for us by small presents of cigarettes, chocolate, etc., and we were able to adopt swaggering poses. The truck took us to a sort of camp enclosed by high walls and containing a few vast hangars. This place was called the Arsenal. A few days after our arrival, and after we had been counted, I learned that there were about fifteen thousand prisoners.

I would find it very difficult to make a sketch of my life as a prisoner. In any case, this sort of thing has been done a hundred times and is of no interest at all. The only special feature of the Arsenal was that it was a transit camp (it was called a *Frontstalag*). We remained there just a month and a half, and nothing in the place was organized either then or later; the whole prison oozed improvisation, ignorance, inexperience, and misery. The French had not the least idea of what slavery was, while the Germans had not yet acquired the habit of victory. They were still stunned by their recent race across France; their hearts were still going fast from shortness of breath and surprise. Furthermore, they were not professional jailers, but soldiers embarrassed by the flood of prisoners they had to keep and rather disliking this work. They left us alone, limiting themselves to guarding the gates of the camp, locking us up every night in our hangars, and making us attend roll call twice a day.

When the gates of the Arsenal closed behind us with a fateful sound, an unexpected bout of despair seized me. As soon as we got off the trucks we were directed to the infirmary hut, where we waited interminably for a medical inspection. As everything was going on in extreme confusion, I had fallen out from the ranks and sat down on the ground, leaning against a partition of planks, my knees drawn up under my chin. I think it was a partition of the infirmary, but I cannot be sure. Only the planks against which my back was pressed still stand up in my memory. One's memory retains only small parts or fragments of reality. Of the big ships in which one has lived only a few ridiculous objects remain. Time takes us from shipwreck to shipwreck, and at each one we have to leap overboard in a hurry, taking with us what falls to hand, which is never what we would like to take.

Leaning against the partition, suffocated by the dust, and oppressed by a sun which shone down with the weight of lead, I gave way to a feeling of desperation. I suddenly realized my misfortune: my life had been cut inhumanly into two. A month before, in Paris, I was living in pleasant and familiar surroundings,

152

enjoying my friends—and here all of a sudden I was plunged into an unknown, hostile world, caught like a rat in a trap, a mere object in the hands of the enemy. At the same time my mind was split into two, and I saw myself in my present wretched condition—a beggar crouching on the ground.

For nearly an hour, everything in me was shattered. I was overpowered, incapable of moving, incapable even of imagining that in a little while I would regain my strength and courage. Circumstances had transformed me into a slave; I abandoned myself completely to slavery. What a difference between this flabby, half-dead derelict flopped on the ground and the spirited youth sporting a rather well-cut blue suit I once had been. The contrast struck me, and I must have reveled in it, exaggerating my lamentable appearance.

These comedies I act to myself from time to time keep me from feeling the sharp impact of events and falling into states of completely disconsolate grief. In a small way, they are like the exaggeration of reality artists introduce into their works. As soon as I heighten my real sadness by adding to it even more sadness, I am cured: the artistic spirit has gained the upper hand, has taken hold of nature to turn it into a work of art or a play. But at the Arsenal it was different. Despair was tenacious, like the grief of a child. A touch of artistic exaggeration was no longer enough. On the contrary, it only made me see my downfall more clearly. I got to pitying myself for the fate that had befallen me, which is really one of the most ridiculous manifestations of inertia and egoism in the world. I pulled a photograph of my father out of my wallet, and thinking of the warm friendship of this splendid being, of his devotion to me and his present anxiety, I broke into tears, something that I had not done since I was six years old.

# XX

## *SHANTY TOWN*

What the Arsenal was during my forty days in it was a kind of slum zone, a Casbah, a native quarter. We lived there, I repeat, in a state of anarchy. Next to the hangars we prisoners built cabins of planks or erected makeshift tents. Paths wound in and out between these fleeting constructions, some of which, like villas at the seaside, were decorated with names, and others, like shops, with sign boards. I remember a small placard nailed to one of them on which the owner had stenciled: "The Cat's Paw." This curious designation puzzled me greatly, but because of some kind of superstition or because the mystery of it discouraged me, I never inquired what it meant.

The Arsenal took on the look of a tiny town, one that was overpopulated and, of course, without women. Although I was very inexperienced, I did notice that most of a town's activities were represented there. A secret and underground life, in which I took no part because I had not been initiated or had failed to find the way to it, animated the alleys, where a thousand trades had sprung up, where foodstuffs, tobacco, innumerable goods, and even jewels, were sold at prices that foreshadowed the black market. Among the more absurd trades were those of the ring-carvers and the belt-braiders. My father had often told me about the liking of the soldiers of 1914 for carving rings and flower vases out of bits of metal taken from old shells. Here at the Arsenal, captivity had produced the same wartime artisans, and their trades flourished. I even bought, for thirty francs, a copper ring, the work of a real artist. The bezel was the head of a lion with open mouth; the whole ring was intricately carved. This marvel was made to measure for me. I ordered it in the spirit of an Italian prince of the Renaissance anxious to encourage the art of Benvenuto Cellini. The ring filled me with pleasure for a fortnight. I do not know what finally became of it. I must have resold it one day when I was hard up or exchanged it for food.

The trade of a belt-braider, on the other hand, always seemed to me close to vandalism. It consisted of cutting good leather belts into very thin thongs and then plaiting them closely. Made in this way, they resembled women's broad belts. I wouldn't have allowed my beautiful belt from Auray to be cut up like this for anything in the world.

Finally, there were gambling dens and, so rumor said, houses of prostitution.

The accident of my four buddies' being sent to different hangars from the one in which I was lodged sufficed for me to lose sight of them completely within a week. For the first few days we felt compelled to meet and exchange impressions—that is, to keep our association going artifically. But we soon found this obligation irksome and our new comrades more entertaining. The ease with which we left each other reveals something of the nature of wartime fraternity and the way in which a man gets comfort after the death of companions.

# XXI

## *SOCIAL CONQUESTS*

The hangar to which I had been assigned was immense. It contained about eight thousand persons who slept almost overlapping on thin layers of straw upon a cement floor. It was hardly better than the open air (there was a roof and some straw, as I say, but the cement was harder than earth), yet after twenty-four hours we had already marked our trails, drawn boundaries between smart and shabby places, respectable ones and the reverse, etc., etc. Our food consisted of a little water and a meager portion of canned stuff. During the day the heat was appalling, the air almost unbreathable because of the dust and various kinds of smoke. Nights were icy.

The population of Vannes thronged around the camp gates, as did families who had come from all the provinces of France laden with victuals for relatives who were prisoners. A complicated system of five-minute passes, of rapid exchanges, of lightning visits, was developed, so that during the whole of the time we were in Vannes we were never wholly cut off from free men. Some of us were even able to get in touch with girls and carry our adventures to conclusion on sacks of potatoes in a shed next to the guard room. These feats amused the Germans, and they lent a hand.

This hybrid life, the easiness of it, the parcels brought in for us, the letters we received—unread by the censor—and the constant relations we entertained with the civilians outside, helped to soften us and to stamp out the last remnants of any will to escape. Within a week a whole network for supplying food and news was organized, and the prisoners clung to it as if it were an essential element of civilization. In short, for people without imagination or courage, captivity as we knew it at the Arsenal was not without its attractions. We were subjected to no labor of any kind except cook-house and latrine fatigues. We spent the day idling in our corner of the hangar, playing cards, strolling around the camp—which was as exciting as a town—taking sun baths near the water tower, building a chapel and then painting frescoes for it, and so on. In my mind's eye I still see the ray of sunshine coming through a bay window across the hangar and lighting the straw on which I slept.

# XXII

## THE EPISODE OF THE MATTRESS

As we struck roots in the Arsenal, our comfort increased. Mattresses appeared. I do not know how, but I managed to get one for myself. A mattress makes an excellent social barrier. It became the distinctive mark of the overlords. To have one seemed to me a greater honor than to have been given the Military Medal.

I had to defend it against covetous fellow prisoners. A corporal of the Foreign Legion, a person to be feared, claimed it one day. He sent me one of his comrades, who challenged me to give up my mattress or suffer reprisals. A boundless fury possessed me. I sent the ambassador back with violence.

Dumfounded at this resistance, the corporal arrived in person to seize the mattress. He was a powerful fellow, covered with medals, and wearing a beard. My anger was so great that I did not let myself be intimidated by his forbidding looks. Besides, the fool wanted to convince me by arguments: he held that mattresses belonged by right to bemedaled veterans, not to raw recruits. The others watched the scene with interest. My honor was at stake—more than that, my future peace of mind. I coldly told the Legionnaire that if he wanted my mattress he must get it. We fought for twenty minutes. In the end I had the upper hand, due no doubt to my indignation. Bystanders separated us, because I would have ended by killing the poor corporal.

When I had calmed down next day I felt a lively sympathy for him and went out to look for him and offer friendship. But I couldn't find him, and when I did catch sight of him two or three days later he pretended not to know me.

When I think back to this incident I tell myself that I was in too great a hurry to beat up the corporal. Everything could have been arranged diplomatically. My comrades would not have despised me for negotiating or even showing the white feather. They would have "understood." They were made in the image of the government of M. Daladier, just the men to litter their private lives with small Munichs and surrender their mattresses, in order to "avoid any fuss," to people who threatened them. As for me, my victory over the Legionnaire, besides enabling me to keep a valuable object, gave me a pride and joy which for two entire days almost made me love the camp, since it had been the scene of my triumph.

# XXIII

## GENERAL L.

Our small community, following in the footsteps of the large ones, clung to any privileges it got. Thus, the rare escapes aroused almost unanimous disapproval: thanks to them we were sometimes in danger of losing our precious parcels, our visits, and our mail. They also resulted in searches which turned the camp upside down for a whole day and led to the discovery of the most incredible things, ranging from double basses to sextants, all of which the Germans mercilessly confiscated.

Communities, like individuals, live on hope. Our hope centered on the signing of peace and being demobilized in the very near future. Rumors bearing on these fabulous events spread through the Arsenal from time to time. Everything was interpreted in relation to them. The climax was reached toward the end of July. During the day there had been a strange visit: a French general had come on a tour of inspection. Formed in squads, we stood to attention in the courtyards. General L. reviewed us wearing a well-cut uniform and surrounded by German officers paying him marked deference. He still had the curt manner of a French general used to taking command and winning victories. He asked us a few questions in the style of, "Any complaints?" did not listen to our answers, exhorted us in a scolding tone of voice not to *make fools of ourselves* (coming from a 1940 general this recommendation has something really magnificent about it), and left.

Despite his blustering bearing, he looked, sandwiched between the German officers, like a jackal in a cage. One could see quite distinctly the terror in his eyes. What was frightening him? Was it the defeat, or the Germans—whose prisoner he also was—or ourselves? No doubt it was us. He saw to it that his escort surrounded him on all sides; all the time he was leaning over to one or the other of his guards, busy and self-important, giving instructions which were respectfully received. This farce, I must say, inspired limitless contempt in us. General L. appeared a vain, wretched puppet. He had good reason to be afraid of us. Without his protectors we might have torn him to pieces. I am sure he had not wanted this exhibition. The Germans had undoubtedly forced him to it, one of their wiles of war.

# XXIV

## *THE ORGY*

It is surprising that after making such unfavorable comments on the visit of General L. we came, in the course of the evening, to look upon it as a happy augury. Our exaltation rose to such a pitch that everybody was convinced we would be liberated the next day. As soon as the curfew sounded and the hangars were locked there began the most extraordinary orgy. I have said that we were nearly eight thousand men in our particular hangar; it was like an autonomous town inside the camp. This evening songs were answered with songs; bottles of red wine and bottles of brandy were dragged out mysteriously from under the straw and passed from hand to hand; an enormous commotion, made up of laughter, exalted talk, the scraping of boots on the floor, and processions in the dark, filled the building. Everybody was moving about. Everyone was making up packs, afraid of not being ready in time in the morning for the departure. Candles were lighted here and there in defiance of regulations. Bull's-eye lanterns and flashlights exchanged signals like ships in a storm. Every known barrack-room ballad was sung and repeated in chorus. One man, who had been in the band, produced a bugle and played "Did you ever know the harlot of Nancy?"

At once two, three, then ten other bugles joined in from all corners of the hangar. Many other army songs sung and played simultaneously set up a gigantic bedlam. The situation was too much for the Germans; they did not even try to interrupt us. They merely lighted the camp to daylight intensity with the searchlights on the guard towers, telling themselves, no doubt, that without arms we could hardly be dangerous. In which respect they were wrong; for on this memorable night of liberation revolvers, rifles, and even a Hotchkiss machine gun with its ribbon of bullets emerged from the straw of the hangar. That gives one to think.

Toward three or four o'clock in the morning the enthusiasm waned, soon to be followed by silence. Next day we could hardly understand why we had staged such a riot. We spent most of the day sleeping.

# XXV

## *ESCAPE*

I think my determina-
tion to escape came to a head at the end of the
month of July 1940. The lack of freedom and the
impossibility of ever having a minute of solitude
weighed more heavily on me every day. I was
cheerful because that is my temperament and because I was young, but I was made desperate by
captivity. I felt this desperation with all the power
of feeling one possesses at the age of twenty. The
idea of escaping came to me in spite of myself, so
to speak, like a defense reaction of the organism,
like the tail which grows again on a lizard who
has lost his original one. Three weeks had been
long enough for the camp to fill me with unbearable disgust. Had I stayed there a year, I believe
I would have died.

At the time, of course, I
believed that my resolution to escape had its
source in my brain, that it was the work of my
will: but I see clearly today that it came also from
farther afield, from my muscles, my entrails, my
nerve cells, and my veins. My body as much as my
mind was possessed by the desire for freedom. I
sometimes think I escaped despite myself, my unconscious being pushing my conscious being by
the shoulders, irresistibly. Perhaps that is what
courage really is.

# PART THREE

## *The Spirit of Contradiction*

YOU CAN SQUEEZE A BEE IN YOUR HAND UNTIL IT
SUFFOCATES, BUT IT WILL NOT SUFFOCATE WITH-
OUT HAVING STUNG YOU. YOU MAY SAY THAT IS A
SMALL MATTER, AND, INDEED, IT IS A SMALL MAT-
TER. BUT IF THE BEE HAD NOT STUNG YOU, BEES
WOULD LONG AGO HAVE CEASED TO EXIST.

—Jean Paulhan

# I

## *OFFSPRING OF THE CENTURY*

My contemporaries sometimes tell me that our youth was ruined, that those who were twenty in 1940 were a sacrificed generation. The war, captivity, the Occupation, the crises and afflictions of that period, robbed us of seven or eight years during which we merely kept body and soul together on empty stomachs and raging hearts. All that is true, but I can never see how my youth was ruined by it. It was a hard youth, no doubt, poverty-stricken and dangerous, but exhilarating; it was a youth of warriors and conspirators which in the end enriched me much more than a glittering youth dissipated in amorous adventures and social successes would have.

There are various ways of accomplishing one's sentimental education. The way of Flaubert's Frédéric Moreau has always filled me with disgust. Yet that represents what today is called "happy youth." Frédéric Moreau *had a good time*. He had an income of his own; he was in with the right set; he had love affairs and spent money freely; he tasted debauchery—

167

in short, he "lived," he "sucked the orange dry."
What a futile way of living it is, this supposedly
"real" life, recalled afterward in middle age with
satisfaction and vain regrets.

"When you have lived as
I have, you will understand that . . ." How many
times this sentence was inflicted upon me. It was
all I heard between the ages of fifteen and twenty-
five, pronounced in a self-satisfied voice by dozens
of incompetents or imbeciles. Having "really
lived" amounts to a few follies one regrets, a few
women one did not understand how to love, a
few companions with whom one was bored, a few
hopes abandoned. There is, in truth, a lesson in
this: how small must be the heart such poor things
suffice to fill.

The French reserve offi-
cers who were thirty or forty in 1940 were almost
all men whose youth resembled that of Frédéric
Moreau. Ladies of easy virtue and pleasure do not
corrupt strong souls, but the souls of the young
middle-class Frenchmen of that time must have
been less firmly anchored than those of their ancestors, since when the war came they were ir-
retrievably lost, incapable of displaying any virtue
whatsoever. Compared with those timorous officers who were anxious to preserve their pleasant
existence and their belongings, the German officers who had lived through ten years of hardship
followed by ten years of tyranny seemed like men
of iron. I do not mean that Spartan discipline is
worth more than Athenian refinement. I am sim-

168

ply noting that France's gentle art of living, the celebrated *"douceur de la vie,"* does not agree with everybody. Some generations favored by nature stand it very well and find in happiness the strength to defend it; others who are less energetic discover to their cost that happiness engenders nothing but fattened-up rabbits whose fate it is to become rabbit pie.

The men of fifty, born around 1900 or soon after, are far more tragic "offsprings of the century" than were the contemporaries of Musset and Vigny a century earlier. Feeling that poor blood flowed in their veins, seeing around them the ruins of a country and a civilization which they had found powerful and had allowed to be destroyed, they too could exclaim, not in anger but in despair, "I came too late into a world too old." Like the men born in 1800, they too had a prodigious childhood, with fathers steeped in the blood of the enemy, with the spectacle before them of a warlike and victorious nation. It is hard to remember today the glory and force of France between 1918 and 1938. They were so great that her children asked themselves no questions. They were children who were too rich, who looked upon their happiness with a pout of disdain. The Great War that our generals won so ferociously, seeing whole divisions perish with iron fortitude, only left these children with an indigestion of patriotism. Their fathers, the heroes, soon began to bore them as war veterans. The rear from which these adolescents watched the massacres had sickened them for four years with its abject boasting—boasting that managed to make the most respectable ideas and men look ridiculous. Everything possible on this subject has already been said. What has not been mentioned is the distant and pernicious influence this bluff had on the youth of the time, the tremendous reaction of cynicism and contempt provoked by the jingoism of the civilians. Skepticism and contempt are nearly always without limit. After the men of the 1922 age group had got over their childhood enthusiasms and made the acquaintance of sergeant-instructors who had spent the whole war in Toulouse, they started loathing their idols and set to work demolishing them.

The poilus of 1914 were fathers whose sons found them too heavy to bear. They had too much glory, and too much official glory. There was nothing left for anyone else. They were ceaselessly held up for admiration. They held themselves up as examples, reflecting the patterns of propaganda—that is to say, reflecting the boasting nature—of our modern political systems which are founded on public opinion. How was it possible for anybody with pride not to revolt against these all-pervading fathers, however great their merit had been? Moreover, after peace was signed, the war veterans lent themselves to all kinds of distressing demonstrations, providing the world with the spectacle of a successful army become old and commemorating its own victories. When they swapped their battle helmets for berets the war veterans stepped down from epic stature to provincial pettiness. They "hung on." Did they really think their mass parades in some way fashioned the policy of France? They probably did, but they were mistaken: heroes are not suffered gladly. For ten or fifteen years these heroes and their ineffectual complaints met with more or less willing consideration, but after that they became open figures of fun. Their leaders died off and they themselves became peevish old fogies. The whole thing ended in making tame and a little ridiculous a very great adventure which will perhaps stand in history as the last act of a victorious and powerful France.

# II

## *BEFLOWERED RIFLES*

The Great War appalled France, left her aghast. She had gone to the uttermost limits of effort; she almost died of it. The mad rejoicing over the victory did not alter the fact that she had been seized with horror. The Great War had nothing in common with preceding wars, not even with the war of 1870, not even with the last campaign of Napoleon. It was a foul war of troglodytes, of Martians and flying men. In 1914 the god Mars had suddenly become a gigantic juggernaut. Beside him Jupiter no longer existed. Mars had sat down on Olympus and crushed it.

It is true, as a matter of fact, in the words of the famous phrase, that there is something fresh and joyful about war (for it is not without attraction for a man who is young and brave to go forth to measure himself against other men), at any rate in its early days, and also in its final days when the victor is elated by his victory and his power. "Ah, God, sweet is war, with its songs, with its prolonged leisures," wrote Apollinaire, who knew what he was writing about and had no resemblance whatsoever to the vile propagandists of the *Echo de Paris* of 1916. But the war was only fresh and joyful for one or two days while the men called to the colors were marching past in their red trousers and the girls stuck flowers in the barrels of their rifles. The following week these vigorous and cheerful boys of 1914, with their beautiful mustaches and pomaded hair, were already dying dirtily in the midst of the cherry orchards. They were going to die like that for four years, and more dirtily still: in filth and mud, tightening their bowels, squatting in trenches, crumpling up under the bombs and shells, suffocating with the overpowering smell of blood and excrement, cutting an enemy's throat with a knife, capturing machine-gun nests at the point of the bayonet, hurling back unexploded German

hand grenades, and still finding some way, even
with broken heads and gaping bellies, to defend
their country.

# III

## *VAUX AND DOUAUMONT*

In 1929, when I was nine
years old, my father took me on a pilgrimage to
the battlefields. I visited the ruins of the fort of
Vaux and the fort of Douaumont and they made
so violent an impression on me that I still see the
yellowish color of the grass which grew among the
ruins. My father had known the defenders of these
places. He spoke of them with such passion that I
expected to see their ghosts rise from the ground
and seemed to hear around me the confused noise
of battle. I stumbled on rusty helmets, on scraps
of metal which had once been shell splinters, on
blackened and half-buried objects which the heroes had used: bits of belt, battered mess tins,
remnants of rifles. My state of mind was like that
of a little boy of Sparta standing reverently at
Thermopylae; I was David weeping on Gilboa.
No historical remains I have seen since, however
impressive, not even the Colosseum or the temples of Paestum, moved me so profoundly as the

forts of Vaux and Douaumont. Standing before these crumpled turrets and these sightless loopholes, I had a revelation of history and of glory and of what posterity is. The wind was swaying the tufts of grass and the brambles. Under the old concrete blocks, now half embedded in the soil, was the perfumed humidity of an underground cathedral. The sum of heroism which had filled these passages was still tangible; I breathed this heroism in deeply, with the odd feeling that it was good for me, like breathing pure mountain air. Religiously I ran through the galleries, repeopling them in thought with the giants who had fought in them. At nine years of age, one's imagination is strong. In my mind Vaux and Douaumont linked up with Valmy and Jemappes, with the cemetery of Eylau and with Rocroy. It was all quite close, and yet it was tremendous, like great, remote historical battles whose survivors had been dead for centuries. The horizon-blue uniform, torn and hardened with mud, seemed to me more legendary, more sublime, than the white jackets of the Royal Auvergne regiment or the bearskins of the Grand Army.

I suppose that the extraordinary exaltation which took hold of me during my visit to the forts of Vaux and Douaumont, a visit that was continued afterward to the famous Trench of Bayonets, the Mort-Homme, the Argonne forest, and Verdun, must be partly attributed to my tender age. Had I been twenty-five instead of nine it would never have occurred to me to waste holidays drinking in historical memories. Besides which I should have belonged to another generation, that of the offspring of the century, of the future pacifists who remained with their mothers while their fathers were away at war. I should have belonged to that generation of the little cads of the *Diable au Corps,* those Cherubinos and storybook heroes whom we see today, aged fifty, at the head of family businesses or as wholesale grocers or corporation vice-presidents. I would have a middle-aged spread, as they say jokingly (that is to say, both a bit of tummy and a bit of experience). I would have a nice bank account, an automobile of the latest model, three children as stupid as myself, and an unattractive spouse whom I feared at home and to whom I was unfaithful outside, on the sly.

# IV

## *A PATRIOTIC EDUCATION*

Thank God, I was nine years old and had the freshness of my age. I was inflamed by the history of France. Napoleon was my grandfather; I cherished Joan of Arc like a beautiful cousin; the Grand Ferré, Philip August,

Charlemagne, and John the Good were members of my family. Vaux and Douaumont, the battles of the Argonne, the taxis of the Marne, were mine, they belonged to me in the same way as my nursery books, my arms and legs, my nails, my hair, and even my silly little thoughts. I felt in some way responsible for them. It fell upon me to pick up the torch fallen from the hands of the dying soldiers of Douaumont, and the idea that one day I should have to resemble these supermen filled me with apprehension.

This was because I had received from my father what must be called a patriotic education, such as, no doubt, few men of my age have received. My father was interested only in France, and the glory of his country filled him with happiness. He often spoke of the war: his accounts, full of exaggeration and zest but also of truth, enchanted me until I was thirteen or fourteen. He was the bard, the troubadour, of an epic poem in which even the comic details, which were by no means lacking, had something grand about them. True, it was always he who was the hero of his stories, but behind him one perceived the long lines of trucks with lights extinct rumbling along the Voie Sacrée, trench mortars spitting fire, houses blown up, shells raining on the Faubourg-Pavé of Verdun, biplanes fighting duels like dragonflies, all the barren Champagne plowed up by the guns, and finally the innumerable hosts of the French army, invincible, made up of jesting heroes, of warriors absolutely like those of the Year Two,* like the Emperor's grenadiers, like the cavalrymen of Condé. How could one but be roused to enthusiasm at the age of nine, at the thought of being the heir to all that, the continuer, the future of all this glory, the posterity of these comrades-in-arms? On Sundays I used to walk through the rooms of the Invalides Museum looking at the arms and armies of France, from Vercingetorix to Marshal Foch, from the spears to the Marne taxis, where everything warms the heart of a small boy and conspires to give him an immense pride. I can have been no more than six years old when I looked down for the first time on the tomb of Napoleon. In my eyes this was the temple and cradle of French glory, the symbol of our greatness and of my good fortune in being born into the nation which had lived this unique adventure. Napoleon, hidden in the center of that big porphyry urn like a kernel in the center of its fruit, like a grain of wheat at the base of a stone, wrapped up in his seven coffins, watched over by a circle of marble victories—Napoleon, for whom a crater had been dug in the middle of Paris so

* *Translator's note:* The year referred to is 1792, since the Convention dated the first year of the Revolution in 1791, when the Republican constitution was adopted. In 1792 France scored notable victories against the European coalition, notably at Valmy on September 20, 1792, and at Jemappes (Belgium) on November 5, 1792. Victor Hugo, most famous of France's nineteenth-century poets, wrote a poem called "To the Soldiers of the Year Two."

that succeeding generations could lean over him as if over a volcano—Napoleon had once and for all placed France above other nations.

# V

## A NEW LOT
## OF OLD
## BORES

You may smile at this "heroic psychology" of a child of nine. But I am inventing nothing. Those were my feelings in 1929 when my elders, those who were two or three times as old as myself, were enjoying themselves with women or with Bugattis, and amusing themselves poking fun at their fathers.

Ah, you men of fifty, how you jeered at the war stories told you when you were twenty by your fathers, still hot from their battles. How they forced those stories down your throats: their feats of valor, their wisecracks, their jokes between two shells, their luck with the girls in the front-line villages, their memories of horror in the fox holes, the cries of their dying friends, their little heroic wangles. You looked with pity at the poor old fellows. How on earth could anyone be a poilu? The peace of 1925, shining with a thousand lights, the Exhibition of Decorative Arts, the Charleston, steel furniture—these realities of life pushed tedious epics into the shadows of the past. The veterans were bores whom the war had thrown off balance: they remained haunted by its horrors and pervaded by its memories. They never wanted to see war again and they did not want their children ever to see the like of it—but they could not hide their pride in it. The sanguinary, sordid story had been the great adventure of their lives. Admittedly, they were a lot of old bores. But here's the rub, you men of fifty: you yourselves are now wearying our ears with your own stories. You have become a new lot of old bores. Only your stories are tales of captivity. Thanks to your kind confidences we know all about the five years during which you waited for the English, the Americans, the Russians, and a few Frenchmen (mostly of my generation and not of yours) to come and liberate you. We know you were gifted for the theater and showed talent in putting on boulevard comedies in the *oflags*. We know you used your leisure to improve yourselves, that the more knowledgeable among you gave interesting lectures, that the more audacious manufactured crystal sets, that you went in for painting water colors, and that you won at backgammon the battles you had lost on the battlefield. How you, in your turn, have forced your adventures down our throats! How well we know them! But they are pitiful adventures. Is it not true that your greatest hardship was to have been deprived of the company of women for eighteen hundred successive nights? What a trial for the former young dandies of 1925! After you got back, men of fifty, you pushed your aberration to the point of wearing a badge of barbed wire in your buttonhole. You promoted this symbol of your shame to the rank of a military decoration. You formed associations of former prisoners of war. I must say that between "former prisoners of war" and "former soldiers," I choose the former soldiers. I prefer them. Tales of war bore me less than tales of captivity.

Naturally, there were honorable prisoners, but it is impossible in a national catastrophe to take special cases into account. It is the general impression that counts, and it is a bad one. Supposing that out of one and a half million French prisoners two hundred thousand did not surrender without fighting: that still leaves thirteen hundred thousand sheep. This crushing majority gives the event its true character. The two hundred thousand men of courage are lost, smothered; they disappear beneath the thirteen hundred thousand unhappy men to whom danger taught no greatness of soul.*

A very convenient confusion has been established between the hero and

* A pretty example of the thinking of the period: A prisoner in Stalag XVII-A was assigned to work on a farm. Every day he took his master's cows across the frontier into Hungarian territory, from which he could have escaped with ease. Notwithstanding, every evening he returned punctually. The reason he gave for this senseless behavior was: "But I had to bring the cows home."

180

the martyr. There is nevertheless a difference: that between the positive and the negative. The hero acts, the martyr endures.* Yes, you were martyrs, you men of fifty, but unintentionally. Your sin was to settle down to this martyrdom, to make yourselves comfortable in it. Your crime was never to have despaired. I remember, at the Arsenal, hearing the theoreticians of captivity argue —while lapping up the greasy water in their mess tins, which constituted their entire lunch—that the only rational thing to do in a war was to be taken prisoner as soon as possible in order to be able to sit out the hostilities in peace and quiet.

You remained prisoners of war for five years: you might just as well have remained twenty years; you would have been prepared to spend the rest of your lives in the camps. Only the first year is painful. Little by little the system improves, discipline slackens. I am convinced that many prisoners left their camps with regret, and that today, faced with the high cost

* What an extraordinary degradation the word *martyr* has suffered. Originally a martyr was a witness to God. Now he has become a passive animal, an ox led to the slaughterhouse by virtue of historical determinism. God knows they are feted enough, these poor oxen, once they are dead. They are victims, without any doubt. But are mere victims really entitled to anything beyond indignation over the crime committed by their executioners? In any event, they certainly do not deserve the innumerable monuments raised to them in France during the past ten years. Will I be called anti-Semitic because I say that the poor Jew tortured and killed by the Nazis is *not Polyeuctus or even Pauline*? That he did not cry out when dying, "I see, I know, I believe, I am undeceived."

181

of living, taxation, business responsibilities, and the nagging of their wives, faced, in short, with the horrors of peace, they sigh and say, "Those were the days."

# VI

## *THE LOST GENERATION*

France, this aged, unhappy mother, this pauper to whose rags still cling tattered bits of the fineries of the past—the frayed fleurs-de-lys, the tarnished eagles, the plucked cock —this parent you have forced to go begging at all the gates of the world, who is being kicked out of Africa and Asia, who is being spat at by the guttersnipes of Cairo, whose last resources are dropping from her rheumatic hands—this France will one day drag you, men of fifty, before the bar of history. She will point you out to your contemptuous and penniless posterity as the men guilty of her misfortunes and the slavery into which she is already tottering. You thrust France into a paralytic's chair which we, your sons, must push. The lost generation is not our generation, it is yours. It was lost for everybody. The nation could have done without you. You cannot even dream how poor you will be in a few years' time. Flourishing men of fifty, you will long ago have sold your automobiles, you will be tired, famished graybeards, having nothing to do in your unheated apartments but chew over petty regrets for a pleasant defeat. It has been said repeatedly that France was betrayed in 1940. Of course she was betrayed. But not by the Fifth Column. She was betrayed by you, men of fifty. She was betrayed by what should have been her vital forces.

# VII

## *THE COLOR OF A BYGONE AGE*

It is rather curious to see how today people take refuge in the past. The period of 1900 is fashionable. It is being revived everywhere. In the past few years there has been a glut of plays by Georges Feydeau in the Paris theaters. The film producers know that nothing has so much success as costume films set in the time of President Fallières.

This love of "the good old days" is not without precedent. It existed during the first half of the nineteenth century. In 1840 most of the light comedies were played in Louis XV costumes and so, later on, were certain plays by Labiche, the portrayer of the *petit bour-geoisie* of the Second Empire. In Balzac there are many references to this taste, particularly in *Cousine Bette*. For the men and women of 1840, the good old days were those before the Revolution, before this sudden break, this gaping precipice, between the old days and the new. The old regime swept away by the Revolution represented a stable society, established for centuries, with recognized values; its last years had unfolded amidst a comfort and magnificence that would never again be known. People were hankering after the great aristocrat personified by the Duke of Richelieu, that superman whose power knew no limits. There were silly regrets for extravagant pleasures pursued by a couple of hundred libertine marquises, in the private little mansions of their mistresses. People gave no thought to the twenty million serious-minded Frenchmen, the artisans, workmen, squires, judges, apothecaries, who led the same dull lives their nephews did later under Louis Philippe. The reading of *Le Chevalier de Faublas,* a delightful book, inflamed these daydreams. After the Restoration, in 1821, Chateaubriand wrote: "You have not seen anything if you did not see the pomp and ceremony of Versailles, even after the dismissal of the ancient house of the King: Louis XIV was still there." In short, people were in love with the color of a bygone age.

In 1956 people are still chasing the rainbow colors of a past age when they grow emotional about the *belle époque*. Yet what a mediocre author was Feydeau and what a contemptible kind of play was the bedroom farce! Contrary to existing prejudice, I do not believe that the 1900 period was lovely; I believe that it was hideous in practically all its manifestations—rather stupid, and certainly very cruel. You may say, But what about the Impressionists and Debussy and Proust? To which I reply, they were the exact opposite of Feydeau and, to stretch the meaning of the term a bit, they were also the exact opposite of the 1900 style. People started reading Proust only after the 1914 war; Renoir lived in want; as for Debussy, lovers of Massenet greeted the opening of *Pelléas et Mélisande* with catcalls.

Sincerely, I prefer the period between the two wars. Women's clothes were just as ugly, but people were a little less stupid. Ask a seventy-year-old workman today whether he thought times were good when he was young: a working day of twelve hours, no holidays, no right to be ill. Despite the beautiful, solid currency with its gold coins and silver five-franc pieces, despite small savings unthreatened by inflation, working people of that time watched with terror as old age came upon them. The ordinary people were more despised than under Louis XVI and were treated more harshly; their middle-class masters were not so good as the aristocrats, who had possessed some nobility of character and in whom a dozen centuries of feudalism had at least instilled a feeling of solicitude toward their villagers.

# VIII

## THE
## NAKED MEN

The past is deceptive. What survives of an era is what its contemporaries did not know about it. What personifies the decade of 1830 to 1840 for us today, what gives those years a characteristic flavor and even a specific countenance, is their Stendhalian *tone* —which most of the people living then knew nothing about, and which was unique. In 1840 France was pedantic and solemn, just as she is today. Thought was ruled by morons whose names have been forgotten. The belated revenge of the great artists against their time is to perpetuate it not as it was literally but as it was seen through their minds, as it was perceived by their exceptional sensibilities. The end of the nineteenth century seen by Auguste Renoir did not resemble the end of the nineteenth century as it actually was. The proof is that then nobody bought his pictures. But the period resembled Renoir profoundly, essentially. For a certain number of people (they will become more and more numerous, until unanimity is reached) 1900 has already assumed the wholly false and wholly true visage of the paintings of Renoir, and not of those of Carolus Duran or Helleu; of the prose of Proust and not of Bourget, of the poetry of Apollinaire and not of Samain, of the plays of Claudel and not of Feydeau.

But, of course, *that* 1900 is not picturesque; it is not "amusing"; it is a timeless 1900 which in the world of naked ideas will join company with the Empire style as seen by Chateaubriand, the Louis XIII style as seen by Corneille, the Francis I style as seen by Leonardo da Vinci. Rodin was right when he sculpted Victor Hugo naked and Balzac in a dateless homespun cloak; he thus drew them out of their time as they had drawn themselves out of it. Proust, Leonardo, Chateaubriand, are naked men, undressed by their very genius—just the reverse of François Coppée, whom one can scarcely imagine without his celluloid collar and his knee-high overcoat, or of Benserade, whom one cannot think of without his plumed hat. Who would dare represent Montesquieu wearing the headgear of a French eighteenth-century magistrate? He spent a good part of his life dressed that way, but eternity has stripped him of his wig and his ruffles, leaving him a bare, brilliant profile. The man of genius is recognized by his ability to show himself naked without appearing ridiculous. That way he joins his peers of the centuries past; that way the era he illustrated is stripped of its superficial fashions and its outmoded graces and even of its historical character.

True, this austere view makes subsequent generations, for whom history is only a question of clothes, feel ill at ease. Whereas Renoir was insidiously transmuting the dresses of the Félix Faure ladies, with their leg-of-mutton sleeves, into sumptuous court dresses worthy of Velásquez and Rubens, and whereas Cézanne with his brush was metamorphosing enamel coffeepots into the silver ewers of Cellini, today every effort is being made to revive those leg-of-mutton sleeves with scrupulously realistic precision and to restore the painted, cast-iron brambles which the decorators of the turn of the century spread so profusely throughout the stairways of our apartment houses. Nobody any longer jeers at the "Metro" style. Rather the opposite: it now arouses feelings of tenderness. What power, what poetry, attaches to these horrors? There was some point in copying the style of Louis XV in 1840 or even in 1875; there was the wish to reproduce a charming form of art. But the transmutation of these vile metal brambles—vomited at and abhorred by every man of taste who saw them when they first appeared—into glorious laurels constitutes an incomprehensible aberration of human sensibility.

# IX

## *A LOST CAUSE?*

It may well be affirmed of pre-1914 middle-class France—cruel and inept, lacking in generosity and taste, a France of top hats and social injustice—that she did not exist at all. That she was nothing: wind; a vain and iridescent bubble. But suddenly this France settled down to the task of living prodigiously and unforgettably when, in the month of September 1914, her children got themselves killed in her defense on the banks of the river Marne. And that was only the beginning. For four years, every month inscribed a fresh name in history and legend. A hundred years after the victories of Napoleon, other battles came to be superimposed on those of Lodi, Iéna, Danzig, and to eclipse them. At last we had a new Austerlitz!

There were other miracles just as astonishing as the taxis of the Marne: from the second-rate political personnel of the Third Republic, still living under the shadow of the Panama scandal, emerged staunch, adamant men; from the general staff, still shaken by the Dreyfus case, energetic generals detached themselves, giants who were determined to win the war that had been offered them and who for a start got rid of the numskulls by sending them to Limoges. France had once more become the reservoir of soldiers of which Chateaubriand spoke with admiration.

Beneath his topper, even the face of Poincaré, with his pointed little beard and his air of a growling dog, assumed some element of beauty.

Clemenceau, a suspect personage who had made his way across the Third Republic coining epigrams, turned himself into the Father of Victory. This overgrown schoolboy, who all his life had amused himself by overthrowing governments, suddenly became a terrible graybeard, the patriarch of France leading his people, like some new Moses, into the promised land of peace and glory.

When Italy left the Triple Alliance everyone was delighted to note that even our ambassadors, and M. Camille Barrère in particular, were men of superior stamp. Sergeant Flick was killed leading a raiding party in the Argonne forest; Croquebol and Laguillaumette brought back his body at the risk of their lives; Lidoire won medals in the Dardanelles. How beautiful all that was. In the midst of this heroism, one could feel free to detest and despise war. Courage was needed for everything, and chiefly for being a conscientious objector. With what ardor I would have sided with the mutineers of 1917 if I had lived at that time! And how I should have cried over Jaurès, assassinated in the Rue Montmartre!

Alas, I never saw France in her hours of triumph. I reached man's estate only in time to see my country destroyed and dishonored, the object of disdain and derision, a doormat for the New World. I am reduced, with my contemporaries, to contemplating our last victory, now thirty-eight years old, as it fades into the past like a very old star fading out of the sky.

A defeated man does not make a good philosopher. Only victory leaves a man with decent pride free to make his choice. Is France a lost cause? If she is, the spirit of contradiction, which denotes the awakening of honor, bids us devote ourselves to her. A lost cause is a sacred thing. Any man who abandons it is the most abject of cowards, the lowest of men, no better than a dog.

# X

## THE GREAT DISAPPOINT- MENT

After they were demobilized and had returned to their homes dressed in their grotesque army-issue "civvy" suits, the war veterans of 1914–1918 suddenly ceased to be heroes. They got back to wives who had either suffered or been unfaithful. They slipped back into a lukewarm, timorous affection. They made the acquaintance of children who had been brought up by their mothers. The mother had become the head of the family. She had won this title, and she kept it. Since the war of 1914, there have been no fathers in France.

Strange and pitiable was the destiny of the soldiers of the Great War. One would be tempted to say that in taking off their horizon-blue uniforms, they left their heroism behind them. In handing in their rifles and their bayonets, in returning their cartridge belts and forage caps to the armory of patriotic accessories, they also stripped themselves of their virtues. Donning their civilian overcoats, they seem at the same time to have resumed their prewar souls, but in a tired condition. All that remained of four and a half years of formidable fighting was an enormous fatigue and an inexpressible disgust at the massacres of the war. They had had too much of it. The veterans of the 1915 age group had become old men. All the soldiers had understood, right from the battle of the Marne, that this Great War had become ignominious. They had set out for a violent and brilliant campaign; they had anticipated three months of *furia francese,* an entry into Berlin in the best Napoleonic style, with drums and trumpets, the trampling of hoofs on the conquered pavement, the dismantling of the statue of Bismarck, and tricolor flags floating over the Brandenburg Gate. This idea was so firmly anchored in their minds that there were soldiers who feared the war would be over before they could join up. My father, for example, who was mobilized in the medical service, at once asked to be transferred to the artillery: he wanted to "see the war" while there was still time, and he wanted to do some fighting, for after all it was an experience one should have had.

He had all the time in the world to see the war, and to experience it, and to become disgusted with it; and others had even more than he. The Great War was a bad surprise for everybody, for the French and for the Germans. Both had dreamed of vast movements, of exaltation, of victorious marches, of immediate and definite decisions. Instead of that, they marked time for four years, they botched the war, creating bleak hecatombs for the sake of taking a hundred yards of muddy terrain. On both sides the heroes were martyrs simultaneously. In the communiqués generals called the troops "aggressive." It was more a case of obstinacy. Four and a half years of obstinacy. Four and a half years without budging, their watchword being: "They shall not pass." Battles were called offensives because the troops facing each other were so numerous. To keep a single square mile of France, as much bravery was deployed as the armies of Napoleon needed to conquer Prussia or Poland. To capture a dead hamlet of twenty houses, where no human being had lived for two years, combats were fought as fierce as those necessary for a capital. How precious France must have been, that so many of her children consented to die rather than give away a mile of her territory. Soaked in the rum ration of attack, doped like race horses, the poilus held on grimly to the national soil, retook it foot by foot with intense fury but with no enthusiasm. They were heroes, but this they did not care about. They had been placed there with the assignment of being heroic, and heroic they were; but it was a point of honor with them to describe themselves as heroes against their will. They were heroes nauseated with heroism.

# XI

## *BACK TO CIVILIAN CHATTER*

When a man has been a gas-company employee, insurance agent, schoolteacher, bookkeeper, suburban gardener, government messenger, or night watchman, he does not settle down to heroism like a character in a romantic or even classical play. It is the other way around: heroism settles on the man like a mortal disease. He suffers it, endures it, puts up with its crises as best he can. He has only one idea: he wants the disease to leave him, the epidemic to be checked. Heroism is like a plague. All around the hero his friends succumb or are crippled. Every morning he says to himself, "Today it is my turn." He looks at his face in a broken mirror: it is an ashen face, exhausted, covered with stubble, ageless. At twenty he looks fifty; he reads the mark of fate on the brows of his comrades and asks himself if they do not read it on his.

Who could be equal to such a destiny? When the soldiers of 1914 were demobilized, they became talkative. For four and a half years they had dumfounded the world without saying a word. When they got home they wanted, naturally, to impress their wives. Fifteen hundred thousand comrades were dead. They had been lucky to escape, and they were determined to tell the story of what they had lived through. They adopted poses when the simple truth was already so great. For years, war stories in France took the place of fishing stories. There also developed the Associations of War Veterans with their claims and complaints, and the War Memorials in the villages—a blossoming of bad art unique in the history of sculpture and the history of France. While our soil was being littered with statues of dying soldiers in cheap stone, Gallic cocks in brass, and weeping angels cast in concrete, the war veterans were reducing their epic to the level of street-corner gossip. How sad to think that something really superhuman has been so poorly perpetuated in art and politics. It is revealing that, apart from some beautiful poems written in the trenches by Apollinaire and some great verses of Claudel's, the war of 1914 did not produce a single epic poet to write about it in terms worthy of the event. It only uncovered a few rather second-rate novelists.

To be sure, one cannot expect men to love war, especially modern war, which is more frightening than an earthquake, a real metaphysical scourge. But there are degrees of horror and of loathing. The setting off to war with a flourish of trumpets and beflowered rifles had roused some small enthusiasm, but once this was over the French soldiers in 1914 took to hating furiously the adventure they had been thrown into. They fought like lions, but they fought with despair and a bitter irony that were the very opposite of the patriotic mouthings attributed to them by the war correspondents and the scribblers of the Parisian newspapers. When it was all over, most of those who escaped forgot the irony and the despair. Memory, with its imitation jewels and cheap paste, quickly decked out the duckboards, the ruins, the mud, the blown-up dugouts, the dead bodies. In any case, if one had told them *everything,* the civilians "would not have understood." And it would not have done to contradict too flatly what had been written in *Le Matin, Le Temps, L'Echo de Paris.* These papers had had the time, during four and a half years, to create a romantic image of the war in the minds of the people of the home front, an image which was coherent and which therefore seemed true. In forgetting the real horrors they had lived through, the war veterans displayed modesty. And, furthermore, time nibbled away at the apocalyptic visions they had seen. Those who had not suffered in their flesh from shells or machine-gun bullets—and even those who were crippled—forgot the livid dawns and the bombardments the way one forgets physical pain. War accomplished its usual transformation. It left in the souls it had conquered only a residue of boastfulness.

Then there are also good war memories: those did not perish. The veterans never tired of talking about their magnificent brotherhood, their drinking sprees in the villages behind the lines, their amusing pranks. At the end of a few years, nostalgia invaded these memories, and the horrors, if they were mentioned at all, became something abstract, something unreal; they no longer existed in the mind except as concepts.

# XII

## *THE FIRST MODERN WAR*

"The infantry, queen of battles." This time-honored phrase was never so true as in 1914. The Great War was won by obstinate foot soldiers who would not budge from positions they had been ordered to hold. It was an immobile and somber war. There was nothing about it of *the festival,* to use Victor Hugo's word. It was an unending watch in the bowels of the earth, in its "intestines" as they used to say without realizing the truth of the image conjured up by that expression: millions of microbes devouring one another in the dark recesses of stinking entrails. The gay charges of Prince Murat, led with clarion calls, the gleam of polished breastplates, and the carnival of many-colored uniforms, were relegated to some fabulous past. Even the attacks on foot of the mustachioed soldiers of the Year Two led by the drumbeats of little Bara, with the music of *Sambre-et-Meuse* heard between the salvos of muskets—even these were no longer the order of the day. War had ceased to be a march. It had become a crawl. It was impossible to slip in *between the bullets,* because the bullets formed an impenetrable curtain. The firing was murderous. The light shells, the "Jack Johnsons," the grenades, the bombs, the mustard gas, the flame-throwers, forbade any old-style heroism, any heroism *à la Française*. The enemy arrived with great speed, shouting *Nach Paris*. He had swallowed Belgium in one mouthful; with one bite he had torn off the east and north of France; and that was the end of it for four years. The infantry of Marshal Joffre in the taxis of Marshal Galliéni arrived on the Marne—a pleasant river lined with dance halls and bathing pools, where Maupassant had gone rowing in shirt sleeves and a straw hat, with which Manet and Renoir had watered the most beautiful landscapes of modern painting—and they transformed it into a huge defensive wall, a new Great Wall of China. There was never any risk of the wall's collapsing: its foundations were solidly anchored to the ground by hundreds of thousands of corpses.

The French infantry won the Great War, but it won it through obstinacy. It constituted a barrier against an onslaught. It fought a defensive and negative war, the war of people who do not want to make war but are compelled to fight by honor and the determination not to fall into slavery. The spirit of revenge animating the French in 1914 did not outlive the battle of the Marne. It was at once replaced by a spirit of resignation, a resignation to being heroic. But this spirit of resignation was more powerful than the German spirit of conquest, and perhaps also more fitting to the times and what Ludendorff very aptly called "total war." The

Germans threw themselves into this total war with the hearts of their ancestors at Sadowa and Mars-la-Tour, who knew only the Dreyse gun and the hand-operated machine gun. It was the Germans who were behind the times. On the Marne they ran into total war, immobile, frightening, which swallowed them up the way an anemone swallows. The Germans found the word, but it was the French infantry opposing them which taught them the thing, which imposed this unprecedented type of warfare, the first modern war, and which won it. With their supposedly invisible uniforms, unlike the uniforms of all past centuries and all past armies, the French infantryman wrote into the pages of history a new type of grandeur, a grandeur hitherto unknown, the grandeur of the infantry, a sort of Protestant beauty.

# XIII

## *SHORT OF A CARDINAL*

It is understandable that in France the Great War was considered the last of all wars, the war to end war. It was the war of progress, like nothing that had happened before. For a few years it was seen as the ultimate convulsion of the old world, the ejection of its last venom, a washing of the old face of humanity with sulphuric acid. Its new face was going to be that announced by Victor Hugo in his hymns to progress and by Renan in his *The Future of Science*. Clemenceau's sad sally about defeated Germany, "We will saddle them with a Republic," must be interpreted not in the sense of a malediction but as the angry announcement of a benefit to be conferred. The Republic, despite its muddles, appeared the only political system compatible with the future.

These conservatives were more optimistic than professional revolutionaries. A Clemenceau genuinely without faith would never have "saddled" Germany with a republic. He would have left it with its old Kaiser, its little princedoms, its feudal quarrels; he would have concluded burlesque alliances with Bavaria or Saxony. In a word, Clemenceau lacked the ferocity and immorality of the ecclesiastic. To remake the political map of Europe we needed a disillusioned cardinal believing in neither man nor science and thoroughly convinced that human nature in another thousand years would be exactly the same as it was under Clovis. But all we had was an ardent layman—generous, no doubt, despite his age, but less careful for his country than he had been for his own career forty-seven years earlier on the occasion of the Commune.

# XIV

## *THE INDUSTRY OF WAR*

The 1914 war did not make a clean sweep of the preceding civilization; it did not abolish the old world. It was an upheaval as great as the French Revolution but no greater. Other wars were soon to eclipse it. In fact, the 1914 war had only dug a new gulf, drawn a new frontier between earlier times and modern, pushing forward the lines of the old world. One was beginning to be familiar with these gulfs, with looking through a telescope at the picture of the "good old days" on the other side. The frivolities in the style of MacMahon and Félix Faure simply took the place of the frivolities of Louis XV. The only notable difference was in the uniforms of the soldiers.

Until 1914, the military man struts and shines. After 1914, he pales and hides himself. He copies the mimesis of animals in the tropics. He advances from the primitive to the industrial. The red Indian warrior, painted and shouting, changes into a workman, an anonymous proletarian operating a machine. His uniform consists of overalls, and war becomes an increasingly difficult trade. The officers are foremen or business executives. Incidentally, who still speaks of the Art of War, as one did up to the end of the last century? This expression is no longer used. It has been replaced by "the industry of war," which means something entirely different. One catches the change as it took place with the slaughter of the soldiers in red trousers in 1914. The old army was stupefied by this slaughter: war was killing its own beauty. The cavalrymen, the pride of the battles of yore, covered their shining helmets with hoods. This detail struck me in my childhood when I was looking through the issue of *l'Illustration* of 1915. At the age of ten, when in my reading I came across such phrases as "truly military smartness" or "martial bearing," they seemed to me to have no meaning, to belong to those stupidities story writers use from sheer force of habit.* As a matter of fact, contrary to the handsome soldiers of the Empire and even of the Third Republic described in the books of Gyp (the last of the alluring

---

* A study of what children used to read in the thirties of this century would be interesting. Thus I, who learned to read from the books of the Comtesse de Ségur, Erckmann-Chatrian, Captain Coignet, Alexander Dumas, for a long time considered those authors to be full of obscurities. Take, for example, the idea of being ruined. Son of a man who earned his living as one earns it today, I had difficulty in understanding, at the age of ten, the despair of those storybook heroes who turned out to be ruined as the result of an unfortunate business deal or some rash act of extravagance. My father was ruined every month, but he was not driven to despair by so small a matter. I suppose all men of my age had similar wonders as children. This was because we were at the point where two civilizations met, on the frontier between the old and the modern worlds; and the latter had not yet produced any writers of children's books.

203

soldiers with their shiny riding boots, their Brandenburg tunics, and their thin, slinky mustaches), the officers and troopers I used to see in the street surprised me by their lack of smartness, not to say their positive slovenliness. They walked about in uniforms which looked more like working clothes, badly cut, from which everything attractive had been systematically eliminated.

# XV

## *THE PHILOSOPHY OF JACK BOOTS*

At the risk of being called futile I would like to say that elegance in attire is as much a source of strength for an army as discipline is. To be worthy of one's uniform does not mean merely being worthy of the nation the uniform represents and symbolizes; it means above all forging a soul for oneself in key with one's fine appearance, attuning the song to the plumage. It can be objected that there are persons who are naturally elegant and others who are naturally inelegant, and that it is no good asking a confirmed clodhopper to display graces. To which I reply that during my short war I never ceased admiring the soldiers' tireless efforts to confer a little distinction on the appalling garments handed out to them at the supply depot. Some made their tunics bulge by pulling in their belts to an inhuman degree. Others made their puttees more attractive by rolling the tops of their socks down over their boots. Still others spent hours finding an attractive way of knotting their scarves. Even the dirtiest and most neglectful soldiers did their best to give their sloppiness an "artistic" look.

It used to be an acknowledged fact that elegance in attire is as inherent in men as in women, that within certain limits it exalts the virile qualities, and that a man is not necessarily effeminate because he likes to be well dressed. The French general staff officers of today are obviously ignorant of this elementary psychology. When attention is no longer paid to these details which great men do not disdain but which small men consider beneath them, one can conclude that the next catastrophe is not far off. Joseph Joubert, the most peace-loving man who ever lived, wrote: "A well-dressed soldier has more respect for himself. . . . He also appears more redoubtable to the enemy and dominates him; for a good appearance is itself a force."

I have mentioned the naïve admiration of the French prisoners for the uniform of their German jailers. They could not get over the fact that simple privates had jack boots like those of officers. Jack boots! What would we not have done, we French, with jack boots! The exclamations of admiration of my sorry-looking comrades in misfortune at each piece of Prussian clothing still ring in my ears; with the French soldiers' preposterous forage caps, their badly fitting puttees, their collarless army-issue shirts as long as nightshirts and thicker than sail-cloth, their coarse trousers reeking with sweat, their prison-made boots, our men felt their shabbiness to the very depths of their souls. The jack boots of the Germans wounded them to the quick. They saw there the symbol of their misfortune; those jack boots represented exactly what they had lacked and what had made the others the victors. One cannot lose a war in jack boots! A man with jack boots is twice a man. The Prussian general staff (from whom the French general staff should surely have borrowed from time to time, without any feeling of shame, if only to turn the efficient methods of the Prussian against himself) has known for a hundred years that jack boots give a terrible impression of power, that even if they do not increase a soldier's courage, they increase his self-confidence and certainly his love for his uniform and profession—to say nothing of his arrogance. A farseeing chief on the general staff could have brilliantly overcome the "demoralization" of 1935 by giving the army jack boots, real jack boots cut from one piece of leather, without laces. They would have been decisive arguments.

# XVI

## *THE PHILOSOPHY OF SLIPPERS*

By the end of the Great War the French general staff had discovered a few principles which were not without importance. Unfortunately there were professors at the Staff College who noted these discoveries, and a complete theory of modern warfare was composed which featured trenches, heavy artillery, the proletarian soldier, machines, etc.—in fact, all the things we had invented under the stress of necessity, egged on by inspiration, and, no doubt, by a genius for war which suddenly rose to the surface from the depths of past ages. But the mistake was to consider this theory definitive and immutable.

The Superior Council of War led France to her undoing by its spirit of logic and its horror of art (considered to be futile). In effect, after 1918, by virtue of the theory of immobile war and the theory of the workman-

207

soldier, tremendous fortifications were built (later proved useless), while at the same time the uniform of the soldier was progressively degraded until it has now become ridiculous without being in the least practical. The change in color is in itself significant: the soldier clad in blue was thought of as coming from a distant horizon and merging with the sky; but khaki, that base color, is intended for the man who withdraws into the earth, who sinks into it, who incorporates himself in the clay, who digs himself in. As for jack boots, they have no place at all in *the system*. Sedentary soldiers who guard fortresses have no need of them. It is surprising that the French general staff, Cartesian, narrow-minded, with its petty logic and its love of trifles (trifles are not the same thing as details), did not distribute slippers to them. Slippers, army issue, of course, described in the manual for fortress infantry, and including two categories: campaign slippers in felt, and, for the inspection of troops, parade slippers in box calf.

# XVII

## *ALGEBRA*

The ideas of the French general staff about the army are stupefying. When it is not thinking in terms of socialistic humanitarianism or when it is not simply being afraid of public opinion, it regards the army as a sort of algebra suitable for solving the equation "war." It is untouched by the human problems raised by the army and by war.

For the general staff it is merely a question of finding the unknown quantity: victory. But with this system the unknown quantity fails to come forth because, unlike mathematics, war is an empirical matter. War is history; this means that its laws are deductions to be made only after the event. These laws hold good for the following war when civilization is not in evolution (and even so, a man of genius, like Napoleon, can throw these laws into confusion), but not when civilization is changing every ten years. The hopeless piece of folly committed by the French general staff was to take the Great War as the model for the wars of the future, when it was merely a war of transition between the old civilization, characterized by slowness, and the new civilization, characterized by speed. During the period 1914 to 1918, horses were already too slow and engines were not yet fast enough.

The general staff was wedded to a spirit of systematization, and once having inscribed the notion of "the immobile war" on its card index, it could never conceive that wars of movement would come back as soon as automobiles and tanks could be used with greater freedom. It did not occur to it that there would be this return to the traditional kind of warfare, exaggerated by modern technical possibilities. It did not occur to it that at the same time soldiers would cease to be workmen and would once again become warriors as in the olden days, and gaily dressed warriors at that. Of all the armies in the world, the French army, constantly one step behind the times, is the worst dressed.*

# XVIII

## BELLA
## MATRIBUS
## DETESTATA

Whenever the general staff is reproached with having allowed the army to die it accuses the Communists of having demoralized it, it blames politics, and the newspapers, and current ideologies, just as cabinet ministers of today explain away our misfortunes by accusing other nations of Machiavellian schemes. All this is laughable and so easy to refute that it is not worth the attempt. I sincerely believe that the Communists have little to do with the demise of the French army; and even if they had,

* It is an old fad of the Republic that it is *immoral* for a soldier to look smart. This notion was being given currency as early as 1900.

that would prove nothing. It was up to the general staff to defend itself. The whole machinery of law and order was at its disposal; all it had to do was add to that a little cleverness. Finally, it is stupid to blame mistakes on others, for in the end it is not the others who suffer the consequences.

It would have been easy to reforge the French army. Troops only prove themselves in war: it is in war that they learn to practice courage; by winning small battles they prepare themselves for winning big ones. The perfect war lay ready to our hand, a people were making heart-rending appeals for help and offering us an admirable training ground. These were the Spanish people. Let it not be said that the war in Spain would have been unpopular. The whole of the French Left, the whole French people, would, in spite of M. Blum, have thrown themselves with frenzy into that war. One hundred and ten years after the Royalist expedition of Chateaubriand, France could have organized a magnificent republican expedition in harmony with her mission and her genius. Such a war would have presented nothing but advantages: it would have enabled us to take the measure of our future enemies, it would have forced the Communists, those army-baiters, to support the army, to give it back all they had robbed it of, and more: to give it back the affection of the masses. The Right would have howled, of course, but silence could have been imposed on it. Had the Popular Front government had two cents' worth of energy, it would have thrown the Right into prison with the enthusiastic consent of the people; had it had two cents' worth of brains, it would have persuaded the Right that this was a golden opportunity to remake an army for France, a fine army, which, once the war had been won, would of course have been an army of the Right, like all armies. There were undoubtedly some honest men on the Right in 1936. They might have understood this line of reasoning. They might well have sacrificed their love of Franco to their love of their own country.

But none of this took place. M. Blum, generous Socialist that he was, had a kind heart and was naturally an enemy of violence; despite his fierce mustaches, in the style of workmen at the end of last century, he had a mother's heart. *Bella matribus detestata.* He hated war, which carries off fine young men to their graves; he knew the vanity and horror of the hecatombs; like the heroine in the tale of Perrault, white doves flew out of his mouth when he talked. He proclaimed nonintervention with all sorts of excellent arguments which history has since thrown into the garbage can. If, at the time, the general staff had been made up of sagacious and courageous men, capable of seeing an inch beyond their noses, they would have forced M. Blum to undertake the Spanish war—a war of our own choosing, a war of conscientious objectors and pacifists. (It is they, as everybody knows, who fight best.) But the general staff was idiotic, it belonged to the Right: to fight against Franco would have seemed sacrilegious—as if that were the point or had the slightest importance. What is more, though one hardly dares say it, the general staff was cowardly. It was enraptured by peace.

# XIX

## *COBLENTZ*

When the peoples looked back after the Armistice of 1918 and were able to see the gulf the war had left behind them, they exclaimed that the nineteenth century did not end in 1900 but in 1914. Four years earlier it had been a world very similar to what it always was, a world living on the old civilization of the horse; and here they were in a new world ruled over by the automobile, a world which no longer smelled of horse dung but of gasoline, a noisy and disrupted world, a Europe in which unknown countries had come into being and in which no one could move about any longer without passports—not to mention the fact of the Russian Revolution, which in one blow had robbed France of her flaming torch.

True, it could already be said that we were no longer the home of revolution—indeed, we were very far from it—but Paris together with London could boast of serving as a sanctuary for all the persecuted men and women of the world, and for all the friends of freedom. After October 1917, Paris changed its mission: it became Coblentz, a home for reactionary refugees. So much effort and so many wounds for such a result! The triumphant French Republic, appearances notwithstanding, had reached the same degree of old age as the Austro-Hungarian monarchy it had just laid low. Thirty-five years later its enormous empire, which France believed could be preserved by giving it the name *Union*, was to break up like Hungary, Bohemia, and Herzegovina. The power of cohesion of empires is always mysterious, and the huge bodies collapse suddenly, as if they have been rotting a long time before they fall to pieces, as if they held together only while they did not move. The first jolt to come along can show the different parts of an empire that nothing binds them together any longer.

# XX

## *THE INCARNATION OF VICTORY*

In the narratives of historians or poets one sometimes comes across an ancient king lamenting the destruction of his army on the evening of a battle lost. Poets have sung the sadness of Napoleon after Waterloo. The old Kaiser going to Holland to weep over the superb divisions we had hacked to pieces and even Hitler going up in flames in Sodom provide an example of despair of which France was no longer capable.

We also had a fine army, the finest in the world. However, that was back in 1923. France was then the first power in the universe. America looked at her with admiration and respect, even with some apprehension. England was already becoming panicky, as was her custom, and looking around for ways and means of "restoring the balance of power" in Europe. Russia was writhing in terrorist convulsions. But France stood there, the incarnation of victory. Great even before the war, she now appeared immense. Everything belonged to her. This formidable metropolis, proudly erected upon its empire, held Central Europe close to itself. French was spoken in Bucharest, in Buenos Aires, in all the capitals and all the chancelleries of the world. We had everything: the loveliest scenery, the finest castles, the best wines, the prettiest women. We were once more on a level with Chambord and Versailles; our past was as light as a feather.

Up to the age of fifteen I thought I was secure in France for the whole of my life. My fathers had reconquered an impregnable territory for me. I would take it easy in their name. I would have tranquillity for the work which, from my tenderest age, I confusedly felt stirring in me. I belonged to that fortunate group which follows a generation of founders, which collects the treasures gathered by the preceding generation and spends them openhandedly. The age of battles had gone by; the age of the creators was arriving, the age of the classics. What happiness to be French and have an artist's vocation! But starting in 1935 this illusion began to wane.

# XXI

## *THE DEATH*
## *OF THE*
## *BLUE ARMY*

All the time I was growing up I saw our splendid blue army growing paler and wilting away; I saw it decay. It did not melt in a furnace as had the army of Napoleon; it was not crushed against a Great Wall of China as was that of William II; it died of anemia. Was it the blood of the fifteen hundred thousand dead that it lacked? No; horror of horrors, the French army died in its bed between 1930 and 1940, it died a natural death—that is, it died an ignoble death, for the only "beautiful" death, the only aesthetic death for an army, is death by violence.

Dying is atrocious after a death struggle in a sick-smelling bed covered with grayish sheets.

The French army had a cancer no army doctor had diagnosed, a malignant growth, a seeping virus, which carried it to its grave and struck it off the list of the living more surely than four and a half years of fighting had done. And nobody came to weep over the passing of that splendid army which had brought us glory and happiness. No Xerxes, no Brutus, no Bonaparte, to express the despair of the nation, to sit down on a stone, in the midst of the ruins, surrounded by a handful of faithful generals, and bemoan its fate. A war lost courageously is a tragedy. An illness is only a petty drama. It is always sordid.

# XXII

## *THE DUAL FRENCHMAN*

With the army dead, shall we ever again see the Frenchman of former days, the Frenchman who did not think the whole world too vast for him, the "dual Frenchman" born of the Revolution, half soldier, half citizen, the complete man, both builder and defender of his works (the plow and the sword, the tool and the shield), the only guarantor of immortal principles? The textbooks of civic education in the primary schools were full of such talk in my childhood. The explained at length that every man of France had two trades, one for peace and one for war, so that we resembled both Athens and Sparta. And they claimed that France was the first country of the world, since its destiny lay in the hands of its own people.

That the people could cease to love their country was something beyond understanding in 1925. One remembered that furious reaction of love for country—the Commune of 1871. France had been abandoned by its ruling casts, but it was caught on the rebound, as it were, by the people, who had not been emasculated by twenty years of a regime which had dishonored every republican. There is nothing so exalting as popular patriotism because it is disinterested, because it is founded on love and honor alone.

The official patriotism of 1914 was very different from that of 1871, and it was already suspect. The war was considered a dirty, middle-class business, and the discovery was made that the real victors were the arms manufacturers, the "merchants of death." The great kings of old, who moved their small professional armies about like pawns on a chessboard, did not conduct ambiguous wars. The hundreds of petty "kings" in the middle-class states are cheating too visibly when they bank on the great popular armies. People finish by growing tired of it. But in 1925 this was not yet clear; it only became apparent much later on.

What an irreparable misfortune it was that the Commune of 1871 was led by such inadequate chiefs (apart from Rossel, who frightened those wretched men) and defended by such poor troops! If the Commune had triumphed and the war with the Prussians been reopened, possibly ending in victory, the face of the world would have been changed for two centuries. The union of socialist republics would have been born forty-six years earlier and Paris would have been its capital. Karl Marx wrote a beautiful, tragic poem about it, full of mistakes, called "The Civil War in France." When one remembers the feats that can be performed by a people fighting for ideas, the stupidity and uncertainty reigning in the councils of the commissars of the Commune drive one to desperation. With even a tiny spark of genius, the men of the Commune would have built us a French Socialist Europe which would have been better than anything we have seen since. And what a pleasure it would have been to contradict Napoleon, who had prophesied a Cossack Europe! We might have been the descendants of Rossel and of our own people; we are the descendants of Thiers and of his hideous principles. That is how we are labeled by the outside world, and that is how we will be treated. As for the dual Frenchman, the citizen-soldier: the bell tolled for him in the month of October 1917, when France ceased to be the fatherland of the proletarians. Nobody will ever again get himself killed for France singing the Marseillaise.

A few years ago I heard this same Marseillaise, now so besmirched, sung by a Red Army choir. The rhythm was a bit slow and the accent semi-Gregorian. To which France was this homage addressed? Not to the one in which I live, alas, but to the one which I could have helped to build if I had been born a bit sooner and if my country had not fallen into such reduced circumstances. Listening to this liturgic hymn I felt like the last believer of an abolished cult, resuscitated for a few minutes by cold-hearted archaeologists, and I felt the unspeakable grief of people who have seen their religion die before they reached the end of their own lives. Let it not be thought that I write all this without sorrow or with the detestable pleasure of a pessimist justified by the event. The very opposite is true. When I write "France is dying, France is dead," I feel that I am writing it with my own blood; I feel that I am attending my own funeral and that I have turned into a ghost who wanders about the deserted Occident. How I wish I were mistaken! How I long to be proved wrong! I would like to shout, "Rise up, ye dead!" I would like to see a new people emerge from our thousand million tombs, from our innumerable generations of affable and indomitable young men.

I would like them to exorcise the illusory monster of historical determinism. But nothing happens, and I remain alone with my funeral cries in the deconsecrated temple.

# XXIII

## *HONOR AND THE STATE*

It is often said that in France the State no longer exists, and it seems so particularly since General de Gaulle has retired. This man gave us the ultimate proof that in any country the State is a matter of character. He held France up on his outstretched arms. Having accomplished feats of honor, he accomplished feats of insolence. Gigantic America, which accused him of being a prima donna, did not frighten him any more than did gigantic Russia. It is stupefying to think that solely by his *inflexibility*, this modest general made despised, powerless France one of the Big Five. For modest he surely was, and even humble, as should have been clear to everyone later on, when he abandoned everything to go live the meager existence of a soldier on half pay.

I do not know De Gaulle; I have never had the joy of speaking with him. I know nothing of his soul except what his acts have revealed; but I am sure that he placed himself reverently "at the service of France." For once, these words regain their true meaning and are no longer simply an empty, hackneyed phrase. I am sure that when circumstances called upon him to represent his country, he put aside his own personality entirely and identified himself with the moral personality of a France which no longer resembles the men that people her but which has not yet, God knows why, completely lost the grave and heroic countenance sculpted for her by fifteen centuries of history. De Gaulle is the only man of our time who can say, "The State was myself." For five years he silenced the man within him; on all occasions he expanded his voice and spoke as more than a chief. He spoke, truly, as a prince. Nothing was too heavy for him; he took on his shoulders all the misfortunes of his country, and he faced these misfortunes as the country would have faced them of old.

Antique language! Obsolete language understood only by other nations, not by France! We ourselves, the men of the resistance, who during four years listened to General de Gaulle with passion and, as I can witness, devoted what amounted to a cult to him—we ceased to understand him as soon as he put foot on the soil he had, more than anyone else, restored to freedom. When we saw him, we replaced love with mockery. We were mediocrities, and I believe we were happy to be. General de Gaulle was making us live beyond our means, and we could not forgive him for that. We did not suspect that in order to change our condition and improve ourselves, we had to begin by living beyond our means.

We took a dislike to the language in which he had addressed us, which had revealed itself as so powerful. The word *honor* was constantly recurring in his speeches. His instinct and his character made him understand clearly how much we had been wanting in honor since the end of the war of 1914. If not for him, France would now have been living for a full thirty years without honor. Heaven knows, he has been laughed at often enough for the heavy and curiously oratorical voice with which he used to pronounce the word, strongly accentuating the first syllable, his eyes sad and cold, his face pale, his look impassive. But then, De Gaulle was not "intelligent," poor man, as Messrs. Pleven, Mayer or Faure were later on. He had merely genius. Honor we found tiresome. We were embarrassed. Repeated again and again, the word made us blush. We hated the thing itself. The Vichyites had left their mark on us. The old realism had restricted them for four years to the rites of a cannibal king, after having made them commit the various stupidities inevitable after an accepted defeat. This realism came back to us, all cleaned up by the victory of other people and shining with new youth. It was urgent, we thought, to give France "her true place"—that is, to drag her down to the insignificant and shameful rank that was rightfully hers. We could not bear to appear to be more than we were. Admirable humility, and typically political! De Gaulle's only crime was to have believed *too much* in France. He wanted to lead his people on to new heights, but the people did not follow him. He was left to climb all alone to the top of his Himalaya and to wave his small tricolor flag in solitude.

# XXIV

## *MAGGOT-MINISTERS*

On history's doomsday I can well imagine the rogues chosen as governors for the past thirty years by the French people—I can hear them cry out before Clio with one voice, "The State, it is not *we*." In effect, that is their tacit motto, never openly expressed but written over every act of our French notables since 1925. The abject Talleyrand, genius of speculation, who enriched himself on the stock exchange and betrayed everybody, managed to de-

fend and honor France in his own way. But today
France has turned into a decaying carcass on
which her maggot-ministers prosper. One cannot
ask worms to behave like kings in misfortune.
Nobody wept for the French army when it died.
It was only one more corpse for the worms to
devour.

# XXV

## A FIELD OF
## ALFALFA

I know it is advisable to
get away from corpses, but I cannot make up my
mind to do so; I cannot resolve to emigrate to
America or Russia, or even England. My country
is the language in which I write, Rivarol said.
But he said it in London or in Hamburg, where
everybody spoke French. And the France he was
flying from caught up with him with giant steps.
The Commissars of the People, dressed in their
plumed hats and their Sunday best every day of
the week, went to the four corners of Europe
recruiting readers for this enemy of the Revolution; they tried to manufacture a French world;
their vulgar and faulty language, their brutal
thoughts, their soldiers' oaths, opened the way for
Victor Hugo. I am not going to repeat that re-

frain about the French language's dying which one reads in the newspapers every week. But it is true that our music is less and less heard in the world, stifled as it is by the glug-glug of the Russians and the gobble-gobble of the Americans. It is true that France shrinks more every day and that soon she will be restricted to her small metropolitan area, walled in by the frontiers of other nations, over which our feeble voice will no longer be able to make itself heard. For a long time I comforted myself with illusions of a universal republic, not realizing that I was indulging in the visions dreamed by dying nations which have nothing to lose by them. But universal republics are made out of blood and steel—not out of gentle mutual consent. It is the conquerors, the Attilas and the Napoleons, who found them. And as they found them on a misunderstanding, these universal republics carry within themselves the seeds of their own destruction. Armies have not yet finished strutting across this planet and pillaging it, dragging their usual train of stupidities behind them. It is no good trying to hide this fact: they will trample France under foot like a field of alfalfa, they will destroy her monuments, which we preserve so carefully, because the molds no longer exist in the souls of our sculptors and architects; and Paris, Paris itself, the city of light, the Paris of Notre Dame and of the Faubourg St. Germain, of the Louvre and of the Place des Vosges, Paris, the open city which they preserved like a curio in 1940, which even the Germans did not dare touch before fleeing from it in 1944, Paris will be ground to dust. At that moment the beautiful blue army of 1925, frightening, deadly as a gigantic electric torpedo, will be only a distant, heart-rending memory.

# XXVI

## *PHANTOM EUROPE*

It is difficult to imagine the death of "Eternal France." Yet everything dies, and perhaps this death is close. France will have lived one thousand years, which, after all, is not bad for a nation. It is longer than Methuselah lived. A thousand years of glory and happiness and tragedy become tiring. France today has almost as much difficulty understanding her past as an octogenarian has understanding the follies of his youth. Can this arthritic old body regain faith in itself? Is this ancient soil still capable of producing those million violent, penniless children without whom nothing great is ever accomplished?

Formerly France shouted at her governments, "Astonish me!" Today she murmurs, "Leave me alone," a request with a dual meaning: no wars without, no trouble within. France draws back into her corner of Europe like her sisters—like England, Spain, Italy, the Netherlands, and the countries of the north. A phantom Europe! It is really strange that no Russia, no America, has yet laid hands on these specters. The death of England, our ancient enemy, is as heartrending as our own. A generation is dying. We become reconciled in our old age. Alas, we have to go. The world belongs to the young. England, France, Spain—memories all—are you going to become the provinces of a future empire? Is that your destiny, is that the world of tomorrow for which my contemporaries scan the horizon so passionately and for which they long, following the conventional belief that the unknown future is preferable to the known past?

# XXVII

## *JULIAN THE APOSTATE*

This faith in the future has always seemed stupid to me, I must confess. The very people who call with all their will for revolutions, the poor and oppressed, ought to be the most mistrustful. Of course, as the centuries go by, the poor and the slaves manage to get hold of a few small guarantees. Social welfare, old-age pensions, paid holidays, socialism, and the trade-unions constitute the only reasons there are for being glad we are not living under the reign of Louis XIII. They form some counterweight to supersonic airplanes and the hydrogen bomb. But these conquests are terribly precarious: the right to strike takes a hundred years to win but can be abolished in a single hour by some tyrant who did not exist the day before; the eight-hour day, fruit of a century of pathetic struggles, is at the mercy of the first event of any serious import, of the first emergency legislation; and so it goes.

I say categorically: I hate the future. I cannot see it other than in the bituminous colors of George Orwell. The future of the modern world is not freedom, as in 1920 one could still believe it might be; it is the police— American, Russian, Chinese, or perhaps Hindu police. And that the police engender war is a well-known fact. In the present state of affairs (but everything changes, of course; everything can change at any moment, there are no determinisms, and human beings are unpredictable), in the present state of affairs, I say, the future, to a reasonable observer, is to be a succession of oppressions and massacres.

I am a pessimist. I admit it. But how can one be anything else? One has to choose between Kafka and Jules Verne. I, unhappily, find in the former more understanding than in the latter. I believe that the world is going toward bureaucratic tyrannies rather than toward the amusing applications of science. My great man is the Emperor Julian, called the Apostate, who harnessed all his power and that of the Roman Empire to the task of recalling the past, of holding it fast, and who died at thirty-two, killed far more by the new barbarism than by the Persians against whom he was making war. Julian knew the price of civilization. He fought for Plato and for Sophocles, for the long-dead Athenian Republic, for Cicero, and for Caesar, and for Virgil. He was a patriot, for what is love of country if it is not an indefatigable fidelity to things dead and gone, to the character these things have created, which has become the essence of a people?

I in my lowly place as a simple individual am, like Julian, a man of the past. I don't give a damn for what the world will be tomorrow if this future has not got French civilization as its foundation. After all, I too am entitled to my small personal idea on the future of the human species, even if it is a sterile and utopian idea. I have every right to want no future for the world if it cannot be created through France. If need be, I have the right to fight for my idea, and I see no reason to deprive myself of that right. My tomorrows sing songs of Apollinaire and Victor Hugo to the tunes of Ravel. The present world, from which France has evidently emigrated, gives us every day an advance taste of a future that nauseates me. I am not resigned to ending my days in the prisons of the puritans of America or the atheists of Russia. I have no desire to bow my head before the idol of historical determinism.

One is what one becomes, and the world is what one makes it, the existentialist philosophy, fashionable a few years ago, used to teach. We shall no doubt not have a world to our taste, I and the twenty or thirty people like me; but at least it shall not be said that we did not try to bring such a world about. To die like Julian the Apostate seems to me the most enviable fate possible. In the actual world, I no longer acknowledge any reason of State to which I ought to bend my knee, be it Communism, Fascism, Westernism, or anything else. I have only one thing at heart, one thing alone clings to my soul as my skin clings to my muscles, and that is an idea of France which nobody believes in any longer. I really am a man of another age; not only can I not conceive the world without France, I cannot conceive that the world might be led by any other nation. I quite see the comic element in such a confession of faith. It would make the whole world laugh if the world read my modest writings, and the first to laugh would be the French themselves. M. Laniel or M. Faure or M. Pleven in the role of the coachman of Europe, like Metternich: the image has something indescribably ludicrous about it. But these gnats, who make the insects of the Third Republic look like giants, may vanish one of these days. Stranger marvels have happened.

# XXVIII

## STRANGE LOVE

It is a strange love that France inspires. It hit me at about the age of twenty-two and led me into all sorts of imprudent actions—proof that this love is a passion. A black-and-white picture of that period remains in my memory. As in certain compositions of Rembrandt, the shadows are dark and tragic but the light areas have an absolutely triumphant gaiety. It is a winter evening in Lyons in 1943; I am all alone walking down a dark street that smells of sewage. I am rapturously caressing a revolver in the right-hand pocket of my overcoat. At last I know who the enemy is and what must be done. My conscience is at peace—a rare thing with me; I am profoundly content at the thought that the petty problems of cowardice and courage, which tormented me three years earlier, have finally been settled. I have become a man, but my childhood is still near enough for me to enjoy my new estate with special keenness.

At that time I belonged to a resistance movement directed by Communists, and I was a Communist at heart; I believed I was fighting for humanity more than for my soil—against the Nazis and not against the Germans. From time to time, however, the idea flitted through my head that these notions of humanity and Naziism were very abstract, while I loved concretely the French and their comrades in battle, and concretely detested the enemy who commanded in my country—that my secret desire was to exterminate them to the last man and lay waste their hateful nation. But it took several months before I fully admitted I was resisting because of patriotism and not an ideology; I needed some time to overcome my shame and disappointment at discovering that I was not a new man but an ancient one—was led by ancestral feelings, not progressive ideas. Even at my youngest age I never resisted the truth; at ten I already submitted to it with joy. Therefore, since my truth was in patriotism and not in any ideology, patriotism it was going to be.

As far as I can judge I was not the only one to feel that way. In 1943 patriotism and Communist doctrine marched side by side, and I have never seen the Communists so happy as they were during the German Occupation. They were being tracked down, they were being shot, but they were reconciled with their heart; they were no longer in conflict with their mother. Their clandestine papers resounded with songs to the glory of France, which they wrote with enthusiasm, if not with talent.* How exalting this Communist patriotism was! I was caught up in it just as they were. Here at last, I felt, was the patriotism of the people, not the patriotism of the rich.

# XXIX

## *OUR BUDDHA*

A strange love, I said. But the fact is there. There are Turks, Rumanians, Egyptians, Brazilians, Negroes, who "love France" without ever having seen it—just for a simple idea which no longer even corresponds to reality. In their eyes, France is the primary value in the world. Victor Schoelcher is still there.

Someday someone must make a study of this imaginary France that is still so powerful, this glorious phantom hovering over the actual France (a small, middle-class nation, cowardly and egoistical, being led to sorry destinies by fools sumptuously installed in the trappings of Napoleon; this present-day France with only a few artists left to give her a little fame—artists whose language she herself hardly

* Talent, and even genius, belonged to Aragon, a sublime poet, as will be seen a century hence.

understands). A professor, or, better still, a poet, should explain to us what it is that transforms the wrinkled, grimacing old face of France today into that calm and radiant countenance of a millenial statue which compels love, which extracts sacrifices, which enflames with a deep-seated fire. After all, I am not stupid, and while no doubt there are enormous numbers of fools among French patriots, there are nevertheless, here and there, a few lucid persons too. Well, these persons and myself feel ourselves wholly committed to the love of France; we are wholly conquered by her deceptive mask; and, commandeered as we are for her service, we adore her. She is our Buddha. She is our Church. It matters little that her priests today are unworthy. With a curious obstinacy we never look at France as she really is; we say, "France, my mother" or "France, my daughter," but never "France, my spouse"!

# XXX

## *WHITE AND BLACK*

I confess that when I ask myself about it (and when I do, it is always without pity and without passion), I do not understand how I have reached this state of fanaticism. For after all, my heart, my thoughts, my tastes, my aspirations, my political sympathies —all these were propelling me in the opposite direction. For more than a year, in 1945, I was very close to joining the Communist party. At the age of fourteen I had discovered Anatole France and the *Canard Enchaîné,* and they had filled me with a horror of war, nationalism, the middle-class order of things, priests, and so on; in short, they had supplied me with the complete guide for the man of the Left. At fifteen or sixteen I had accurately judged the foolishness of Colonel de la Roque. In 1939, I saw, with indifference and irony, war declared, and was exasperated by the state of mind prevalent in the middle-class set from which I came: all this talk about "splendid soldier," the "brave little French woman doing her bit as an army nurse," etc. Politics and the fate of nations hardly interested me. I considered myself an artist—a vocation which, I suppose, must have been strong, since it overcame every sort of discouragement (and even the most dangerous kinds of encouragement), and which prevented me from seeing absolutely anything except art, which knows neither frontiers nor contingencies. The patriotic education my father had heaped on me, my emotions as a child when faced with the memories of history and the war, had all been obliterated. What did it matter to me whether France was victorious or defeated? I would build my own work in any case. The Prussian armies in 1871 had not succeeded in drowning the voice of Flaubert, reading aloud to himself the latest pages he had written. He hardly stopped writing for a quarter of an hour to watch them go by.

When at that age I happened to contemplate my own times, what I saw was a flourishing and stupid France, an apparently powerful State that was flooding us with a stream of indecent propaganda. To me France looked like a giant Narcissus occupied solely with self-admiration. The cinemas showed devastating documentary films dealing with our "achievements," glorifying the French nation; there was much talk about *our* navy, *our* empire, about the honor of serving, about duty. The voice of the cabaret singers broke with emotion when evoking the pennon of the Foreign Legion. The nationalism which sprawled over most of the newspapers revolted me as being in the worst possible taste; when we were so powerful and pleased with ourselves, the most elementary modesty forbade us to shout aloud that France was the first country in the world. I had even conceived a dislike for French culture, a culture which remained obstinately ignorant of all other cultures and naïvely believed itself the only one of importance. This culture seemed to me very narrow—and blind, into the bargain. I read the Russian novelists with passion. These were the thoughts and feelings of an adolescent, but that adolescent was myself. I was all white, and today I find myself all black. What has happened?

# XXXI

## *THE STIFF*
## *COLLAR*

Well, what has happened is that we have been defeated, what has happened is that I have grown older, and that the spirit of contradiction resides within me. The France of 1938 was still living on the ideas and conventions of 1880, ideas with which I was poisoned, which I hated, and which were personified for me by the horrible style of decoration prevalent at the end of the century. Everything was well ordered, everything was in its place. The rich despised and feared the poor, middle-class apartments were filled with tasteless pictures and crammed with velvet hangings, employers fought their workmen, fathers forbade their daughters to go to the movies, at eighteen the boys of good families joined the Royalist party, and young girls defended their virtue with the same arguments their grandmothers had used.

Today all that has been swept away. Everybody has become anticonformist. A tragicomic situation! The bourgeois, the academicians, the soldiers, the nursemaids, the reactionary members of Parliament, the prime ministers, have stolen my part from me. They play it badly, abominably, but they do play it. And, like all bad actors, they shout very loudly.

How can one be anti-conformist at a time when and in a country where the generals start by running down the army and end by losing their battles, where the academicians make mistakes in French, where the newspapers of the Right no longer dare be nationalist, where all categories are confounded to such a degree that we have judges publishing obscene poems and daughters of barristers singing in night clubs?

There was courage, before the war, in being anticonformist, for one was then attacking a strong central power which knew how to defend itself; one was attacking an established order of things. But today? What order of things is one attacking? For the past sixteen years, thanks to the actions of our successive governments, we have seen everything in the way of lunacy that disorder can bring about: prisoners of war regarded officially as heroes, vanquished generals carried in triumph, classes of cadets afflicted with the names of our defeats, and so on. What merit is there in being antimilitarist in France in 1956? It is too easy: France has been beaten everywhere.

However much I might wish to, I cannot reason the way I did twenty years ago. In 1935, with her institutions, her cabinet ministers, her soldiers, her severe court of justice, her sparkling navy, her strict prefects, her Pacific empire, her cruel colonists, and her State patriotism, France was a lion. To tease a lion or stab it with pocketknives was noble and courageous. One ran the risk of being butchered. One sometimes was. But the France of 1956 is a weak and divided country. The anticonformists are donkeys kicking a dying lion. I cannot make up my mind to act the donkey—not consciously, at any rate.

Disgusted with disorder, I am driven back into the stiff collar. This is a position well calculated to result in my being called a weathercock by people who cannot bear anyone to go back on the trivialities of his youth, or, rather, who want him to remain unchanged in a changing world. Nevertheless, it is now disorder that worries and inconveniences me; the experience of disorder leaves me with nothing but extreme boredom and the dislike of having to waste time fighting it and preserving myself from it. I won't even speak of the constant exasperation produced in a man of good sense by the confusion of values and the use of that confusion by idiots.

France now affects a detestable manner: the artistic manner—that is to say, the manner of the bad artist, the eternal Bohemian, with all that that manner implies in the way of the ridiculous and the stereotyped. For true artists live like office clerks or like viscounts before the French Revolution. The whole of

France leading the Bohemian life! I would like to know what Flaubert (who, in his château, in which he played the country squire, vituperated against the middle class) would have to say about all this. France is one gigantic Madame Bovary, an enormous ninny in the arms of Bohemia; her Rodolphe is Jean Cocteau, the acme of the artistic type. But in throwing open the doors of the French Academy to him, she has ended by marrying the fellow. It is the destiny of these Bohemians to marry crazy old widows whose money, inherited from respectable husbands, has not been entirely wasted on bad paintings.

# XXXII

## *LOVE COMES FULL CIRCLE*

The spirit of contradiction is a good thing in itself; and so is the experience one acquires in watching the years flow by and observing the actions of one's fellow men. But these are not enough to beget love; still less, passionate love, which is blind, fanatical. The truth is that France seeped into my bones and sinews, by osmosis.

As soon as she became unhappy, as soon as I saw this giant felled, I recognized her as possessing all the virtues I had previously denied her. I became aware of the enormous loss her fall would be to humanity and, in consequence, to myself—mirror and microcosm, simple little fellow of my time that I am. What started to gnaw at my vitals was something like the posthumous remorse that must be felt by unworthy sons the moment their fathers have drawn their last breath. Everything is fixed forever; everything is now irreparable. The sorrow inflicted, the brutalities, insults, disappointments, lack of feeling, leave the old heart of the dead man; they implant themselves in the young heart of the living man and poison it. The person you have made to suffer, whose love you have so misused, of whom you *were sure,* whose devotion it was impossible to exhaust—this person is no more. You would like to sob in his presence, to display shining repentance, to give him as much love, patience, solicitude as you caused him grief; not so much to hear him say that he forgives, for he has certainly forgiven, but to prove to him that you are no longer the same man, that you bring him a new soul, that at long last, although too late, you are able to offer him the happiness he was deprived of up to the end. Alas, you have before you nothing but a deaf, dumb, blind object, a dead body which leaves you face to face with your own despair, which bequeaths you to yourself.

It is then that a curious search begins. You plunge into the papers of the dead person, you scrutinize them, you write the story of his life, you look endlessly and sadly at old photographs, you try to understand your father's acts and his works. You are suddenly aware that you are flesh of his flesh; the stranger of yesterday had the same blood you have. What an extraordinary discovery! What used to make you impatient with him now makes you proud. This extinct life once had a complexity and richness similar to your own. A multitude of thoughts and feelings which you believed belonged uniquely to you have their roots in him. As the years go by, you become more and more like the dead man. The same wrinkles, the same look, the same manner of walking. Sometimes it is he who appears when you accidentally look at yourself in the mirror. The root has flowered. Love has come full circle.

Something like this happened to me with France. I do not in the least claim that there is anything rational in it; I limit myself to describing a phenomenon of which I was the center. And here I am today unrecognizable in my own eyes, embodying to an extreme degree everything that horrified me eighteen years ago. Here I am turned completely upside down. But the world too has turned upside down. The world and I have each of us revolved, but in opposite directions, and we find ourselves in the same position of antagonism as we were before.

The world was black and I was white. Today the world is white and I am black.

I remember that during the German Occupation a play was put on called *From Joan of Arc to Philippe Pétain*. Today this title assumes a significance it did not have then. In those two names it sums up six centuries of ascension. With Joan of Arc, France placed her sandal on the first rung of Jacob's ladder. With Pétain, she saw that the ladder was leaning on nothing, and she fell dizzily from a great height. I was twenty at the time of this memorable fall. At nineteen I was still a citizen of the Republic of the Rights of Man, that martial, peace-making, colonizing republic. At twenty-one I discovered myself to be a subject of King Charles VII. I had slipped back six centuries. That counts in the sentimental education of a man. When I added to this ten or fifteen years of reflection on the subject (I have always been a little slow), I realized that my heart had completely changed. It was now the heart of a subject of Charles VII, bleeding from a thousand wounds, calling with all its will for a little seriousness and a little glory, hating with all its force the frivolous anarchy of its country and its times. Out of my hatred this book was born. I have called it *The Taxis of the Marne,* the name of the most glorious—and the least miraculous—feat of the twentieth century.

# ABOUT
# THE
# AUTHOR

JEAN DUTOURD *was drafted in 1940, at the age of twenty, and taken prisoner soon afterward. He escaped by jumping off the train on his way to Germany, and joined the Resistance Movement. In 1943 he was caught by the Gestapo and sentenced to death; but again he escaped and resumed his underground activities, which included publishing newspapers in defiance of the Occupation authorities. He ran a French radio program for the B.B.C. in London for three years and still broadcasts weekly in France. He also—in addition to writing his books—is a columnist for a Swiss paper, a movie critic, and an editor for the firm of Gallimard, of Paris.*